KASHMIR:
DESOLATION OR PEACE

Majid A. Siraj

MINERVA PRESS

LONDON
MONTREUX   LOS ANGELES   SYDNEY

First published 1997 by
MINERVA PRESS
195 Knightsbridge
London SW7 1RE

Printed in Great Britain by
Antony Rowe Ltd, Chippenham, Wiltshire

KASHMIR:
DESOLATION OR PEACE

Dedicated to all those martyrs of Kashmir who laid down their lives for freedom and honour.

FOREWORD

No reader will be able to ignore the depth of human suffering at the individual and family level, nor the injustice on a vast scale, that this book describes. Its publication will draw necessary attention to a dismal episode in the aftermath to the demise of an empire. Hopefully, wider dissemination of knowledge and the stimulus to debate the issues, dispersing ignorance, dispelling indifference, will lead to the removal of the causes of suffering and the eradication of its dire effects.

The passion and compassion of Majid A Siraj animate his choice of words and style of writing. They vividly reflect the dedication and commitment he has given to the pursuit of justice for his beloved Kashmir. Agonising over the contents of this work, he has devoted himself selflessly and wholeheartedly to the cause of human rights in Kashmir for many years. His ultimate goals have been the elimination of abuses and the attainment of natural and social justice, with peace, for his homeland. It has dominated his life. His single-mindedness is like a comet in the night sky.

For the above reasons, and because Majid A. Siraj himself writes of his "six long decades" in search of "a blend of piety and peace" (page 201), it would be appropriate to conclude these few commendatory remarks with two profound prayers. The first is from a Hindu source and the second of Islamic origin:

OM. Shanti. Shanti. Shanti.
  Asato maa, sad gamaya.
  Tamaso maa, jyotir gamaya.
  Mrutyo maa, amritam gamaya.
    OM. Shanti. Shanti. Shanti.

OM. Peace. Peace. Peace.
  From untruth, lead us to truth.
  From darkness, lead us to light.
  From death, lead us to immortality.
    OM. Peace. Peace. Peace.[1]

O Lord! Let (our) entry be
  in truth and sincerity,
And let (our) exit be
  in truth and sincerity,
And grant (us) from Your presence
  an authority to support (us).[2]

Dr David G. Bowen
Bradford University

---

1   From the *Brihad-aranyaka Upanishad*, 1, 3, 28.
2   As rendered into English by Dr Hasan Askari, in his *Alone to Alone*
    (West Yorkshire, Seven Mirrors Publishing, 1991), p.84.

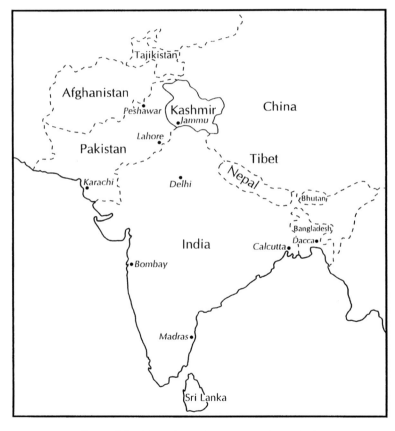

Geopolitical location of Jammu and Kashmir

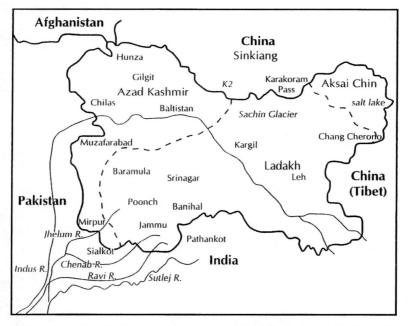

The broken line indicates how the control of Jammu and Kashmir is divided between India, Pakistan and China.

CONTENTS

INTRODUCTION
Shadows and Hopes

'Kashmir', for the sake of compendious description and convenience of text, will denote the whole state of Jammu and Kashmir including Ladakh, Gilgit, Hunza, Baltistan, Kishtawar, Poonch, Mirpur, Muzafarabad and parts of Jhelum, a polity as it existed in early October 1947.

An attempt has been made to interview as many senior Kashmiri citizens and political leaders as possible, in order to corroborate the events in the history of Kashmir with relevance to present day situation. Facts and figures about the political background, with intricate research into the literature and study of the political metamorphosis from medieval times, have been put forward. The hope is that it will clear the mist from the minds of many of those who are lost in the maze of a future for Kashmir.

The book is not intended to be a text for the history, geography or economy of Kashmir. Each one of those subjects would take many volumes like this to chronicle in detail. I have tried to extract relevant facts from the literature and slot them into the perception of a melange of political factions in the story of Kashmir. My own observations have come from the experience of growing up both in downtown slums and elite parts of Kashmir. My interaction with the poor and rich alike, consorting with professionals and business circles and having visited and worked in remote parts of the state, helped me to observe prevailing political atmosphere and over the years a mutation in people's minds. I lived through violent armed repression of despotic rule and its continuance afterwards. I also saw better days in

Kashmir, enjoying holidays in my Gulmarg huts, golfing, angling, trekking, skiing, ambling through club fraternity and societies of Kashmir. That experience has made it more difficult for me to live in exile.

My mind is scarred with events of my childhood. I see human blood splashed and guns blazing, as soon as I close my eyes to sleep. A general surgeon all my working life, I have no qualms about blood But incidents engraved in my subconscious surface like bubbles from melting lava. We lived next to the city police station in Zaina Kadal, Fourth Bridge, Srinagar. It was about 1945. I saw through the glass panes of my closed window, my ten year old playmate walking on the desolate street carrying a bunch of pears in his shirt folded up. Two shots were fired at him from the truck which stood below my window. I saw him drop in a puddle of his bright red blood and the strewn pears. The hostile Dogra army fired at people who were pelting stones at them. The pears were mistaken for stones! I stood impassively, stunned and cold. I could not even cry. I was carried away from the window by my mother.

Children these days are growing up in a war culture. They play with ammunition instead of toys and know how to jump over the fences to run when chased by an army pointing guns at them and ready to shoot. The driving force behind this book has been the cries of anguish coming from bereaved families and those very young boys waving arms and shouting slogans of freedom. Their words come out in an innocent lisp. "Freedom," they said. Looking at them you could either despair or explode. For now, I took refuge in my word processor.

Oh! Where art thou my Lord

And canons of thy laws?

Why make Kashmir alluring

Let those savages foraying

This exuberance your creation

your children and thy nation

The fate of your promised land

forlorn steppes, desolate sand

Enough of blood, tears and pain

Not their folly, nor their bane

Deliver Oh God! from perdition

Forgive their cries for salvation

Amen.

Majid Siraj

Some say 'They want to create desolation in Kashmir and call it peace!' It is after all the native population who make it difficult for the ruling chieftains, because they are in the way of the smooth running of the place. Without people, the paradise could be an ultimate place of bliss for them, all to themselves. The other course would be to subvert them to complete obeisance.

The Kashmir dispute has been a bane in the subcontinent of Asia, causing suffering in all its communities. The people of India have been mired into the politics of power using Kashmir to stir their emotions. Her leaders are not vanquished, regardless of the hectic military activity in the meshes of Kashmir. Indian and Pakistani nationals have lost vital resources and men, fighting wars in Kashmir. Kashmir cannot be an asset to any country in the way it is sought, especially after goodwill has evanesced from the scene altogether. Finally consigned to its fate, this celestial paradise may, one day, provide happiness to a lot of people.

The subject of 'Independence for Kashmir' has been evaluated, with separate chapters dealing with different aspects of its basis and metaphysical analysis. The history, geopolitical background, cultural disposition and economic resourcefulness have been described at some length. The proponents of the accession of Kashmir to either India or Pakistan have argued that on its own Kashmir cannot survive and that food and essential commodities will be in short supply. It is landlocked and will remain subservient to its adjoining countries for access to the outside world. The debate goes on, with both sides of the argument surging ebullience and conflict.

There is a political and military impasse. Two deadly wars between India and Pakistan did not solve the dispute of Kashmir and now an armed uprising has resulted in Human Rights abuses of colossal proportions. The ten million people of the troubled state are in the battlefield fighting for survival with whatever means available to them.

The central theme of this book is an exercise to evaluate the origins, development and the personality of a Kashmiri and his odyssey through a millennium of purgatory. Torn between tyranny and freedom, the civilisation remains extant. The story of Kashmir is full of remorse and yet the rapidly changing political circumstances were fundamental for the emancipation of the society as a whole. The spectre of freedom and peace has always haunted people. Peace is indivisible, peace is the life of their nation, peace is what the people of Kashmir have never been allowed. Today, when the cold war is over and the rest of the world is a better place to live in, the people in Kashmir struggle through the depths of despair and turmoil, even worse than ever before.

Three major countries, China, India and Pakistan stake their claims in Kashmir. They have committed their armies into the depths of the state and have fought deadly wars over its territory. The argument has created a turbulence in the whole of the subcontinent. The real issue here may be territory or a foray for natural resources or privileged defence strategy, but the Kashmir problem remains an insoluble obstacle in the crossfire of a race for power between big countries. Over the years major wars were fought. Meetings to settle differences were tainted with recalcitrance and suspicion. They always responded to each other with antithetical diatribes.

Kashmir, as a nation, is turning an important corner. Its newly found nationalism has gripped the people and become a factor in its theories and practices. It has given rise to subjectivism and an evaluation of its elements. I will leave it to the reader to determine what the best way forward for Kashmir is.

Majid Siraj

GEOPOLITICS

Fossils Under Ashes

Kashmir is a conglomerate of many geological entities. Its origins have been a fascinating subject for conjecture, and various hypotheses have been propounded by different sources.

Millions of years ago enormous tidal waves arose from the Indian Ocean and layer after layer of silt and rocks were deposited to make the Himalayan and Pamir mountain ranges. The rock formations confirm the presence of layers of deposits. The euphemism of this theory has a sinister resemblance to Kashmir's political history! The waves from the Indian Ocean explain the presence of water and rocky mountains. The receding water left shores which are the infertile foothills and the shelving shores of inland sea.

The waves also represent the human tempestuous invasions which hit Kashmir and left their marks. The first people who ever lived in Kashmir had homes in water – indeed, some still do! Islands of land surfaced in due course and people migrated to land.

One theory has been postulated that Kashmir was an expanse of water as part of the ancient globe. A massive volcanic eruption made a crater in the mountains and drained water from the big lake, surfacing land for habitation. Earthquakes in Kashmir are common and the by-products of ash from larva are present in the mountains. Another theory is that Kashmir was an ice-age lake, like one big glacier. The earthquake split open a gorge, ice melted and drained, surfacing land.

According to Hindu mythology the big lake (Satisar) was inhabited by snake people (Nagas) who, fearing the demon (Jaladeo), pray to Kashyap (the Sage) who goes into long penance to deliver the Nagas. Shiva (Hindu God) came down and with a hard blow created a crater in the mountains which drained the water and the earth surfaced on which people started living.

The legend also relates the story of King Solomon. It his been suggested that Solomon drained the water of the big lake by ingenious canalisation. He helped to settle people from far-off places.

Whatever it was that created Kashmir, it has since been awfully serpentine, ruefully demonic and suffered gusty blows from the mighty waves of mordant politics.

Kashmir is a composition of a heterogeneous series of valleys and gorges, steep cliffs and daunting precipices, tucked in the foothills of the magnanimous mountain ranges. The Karakoram is a stupendous and awe inspiring range in which the K2, or Mount Godwin Austen 28250 ft stands out. Kashmir has a distinct geographical identity. The luscious green country is roofed over by the Pamirs on the north-west border, sheltering it from the eyes of the white bear! The tortuous defiles of majestic mountains demarcate boundaries with Sinkiang, China and Tibet to its north-east and Tajekistan (former USSR) and Afghanistan along its north-western borders. The indo-gangetic plain comprises India and Pakistan skirting along its southern aspect, completing the circle of the mighty countries surrounding Kashmir. The countries are intimidating and too close for comfort.

It may be stated that all these countries over the years have fought wars of attrition in Kashmir, much like a 'rag doll' pulled apart by duelling canines. Unfortunately for Kashmir, the game is not over. Kashmir's status never got settled *de jure* by either UN intervention or negotiations. In January 1949, 57,000 square miles of the state were with India, 32,000 square miles with Pakistan. China seized from India 12,000 square miles of Aksai Chin, a part of Kashmir state. Pakistan ceded land to China for the silk road with an agreement that when the dispute is settled the land will be re-negotiated. From 32,000 square miles with Pakistan, 27,000 square miles formed the Northern Areas ceded by British officers to Pakistan. In 1947 Major W. Brown hoisted the Pakistani flag in Gilgit. The Gilgit agency included Astor, Skardu and Hunza. 5,236 square miles are administered by Azad Kashmir. The position today is the same, China has the north-east sector called Aksai Chin, the western areas are Azad Kashmir (Pakistan) and the rest of the state is under control of India. The only de facto compromise struck with China, was where the 12,000 square miles of Aksai Chin were conceded to them by India. Aksai Chin was an integral part of Kashmir. China wanted it because the road between Xinjiang (China), and Tibet runs through it. In return for Aksai Chin, China conceded parts of Arunachal Pradesh, south of the Tibetan border, but that territory is not in Kashmir. It is in India. Likewise Pakistan conceded the area covered by the silk road to China.

Millions of years of His creations, ancient trees, lush green meadows, mighty glaciers standing proud of the slopes, stratospheric snow-capped peaks touching the skies and overlooking a majestic carpet of trees, have left people of the world exalted. The four hundred year old oak trees, the ancient and massive chinar trees stand out from the gardens and wayside. Some of these have been sacrificed.

People of Kashmir in recent years are traversing the choppy oceans of politics and experiencing frightening tides, tall and gruesome, hiding the view of the horizon. Kashmir has been the place of learning and the Buddhist and Sanskrit scholars made a mark in the contemporary literary world. The ancient treasures in shrines and temples have been mercilessly vandalised over the years of changing rule and prevailing ignorance of their value.

Inside the Shalimar garden during Shah Jehan's time the black marble pavilion was gilt with Persian inscriptions saying 'if there is paradise on earth, it is here, it is here.' The grey stone mosque built by Mogul prince Dara Shikoh near the Hari Parbat fort, and at the gateway to Nagar town built by Akbar are both reduced to ruins. The Pather Masjid stone mosque built by Nur Jehan still stands, thanks to political rallies and its constant use for prayers.

Kashmir is a point where central Asia, east, west and south Asian countries meet, with seventeen known exit routes leading in and out through mountain passes. Central Asia extends from Badakhshan in the west through Dushanbe, Samarkand and Bokhara to Kahgar,

Yarkand and Khotan in the east. Tajekistan and Russia can peep over the verge of Pamirs. The west borders with Afghanistan and the land of Pathans. It is the southern borders with India and south west with Pakistan where the main arteries of communication to the outside world are, and through which most of the recent troubles for Kashmir have been wheeled in.

Kashmir, it can be surmised from its geography, is very vulnerable to advances from its predacious neighbours. For thousands of years the mighty mountains encircling its perimeters have only been a feeble barrier to defend its territorial integrity. Inevitably the Himalayan backwater has been violated by unscrupulous invaders from all sides.

The foothills of the Himalayas, the rugged contours of the Karakoram range, the awesome glaciers, the lush green meadows and exquisite monuments of Jammu and Ladakh make this terrestrial paradise the envy of the world. It is so beautiful that even those who only breeze in for a holiday fall in love with it.

The British left India in 1947. The Indian people inherited abject poverty, rampant disease, and the effects of overpopulation. The split into two nations culminated into roadside orgies of slaughter between Hindus, assisted by Sikhs and Muslims. In most of the cities of India, human blood and flesh could be seen strewn across the streets. Millions became refugees in their own country. Chaos and anarchy were the norm. People swarmed into trains and refused to pay fares. "We are free people now," they said, "this country is ours, we do not pay." Hatred and strife over caste, religion, territory and property dominated the political scene. In all this chaos, 'Kashmir' stood out as an example of peace and harmony between religions, a "beacon light" of hope for India to see. (Mahatma Gandhi.)

India and Pakistan, as nascent independent nations, were just getting to grips with administration and governance and coping with the maelstrom of ethnic riots when both countries became embroiled in a fight for the annexation of Kashmir. Leaders with vested interests in Kashmir were exhibiting their shining armour and surreptitious games were played. In the ensuing rampage and disorder, some leaders made decisions based on emotion and rash diplomacy. In the middle of this disarray in the whole region, Kashmir became a nidus of activity and the whole subcontinent was torn apart with destructive wars fought to acquire the territory of Kashmir. Both India and Pakistan were spurred on to fight more wars by arms-exporting countries.

Roads to the Outside World.

Kashmir as an independent nation cannot survive isolated from the surrounding countries and the outside world. This has been an argument with independence sceptics: 'in time the place will implode into devastation, chaos and starvation. It will be choked out of its polity and merge as a vassal state with another country.' Communication by means of road is mandatory to survival. The first road ever built was between Kohala and Kashmir in 1888. The road claimed many lives with men falling over the cliffs and getting snake bites. Rope bridges were constructed near Uri to span across the gorges. The crossing was so frightening that some people were blindfolded, bundled into a sack and taken across as a load.

Allegorically speaking Kashmir has been likened to a multi-storey house. The first storey is reached by climbing 8,000 ft mountains from the level of the plains. The rooms inside are Kishtawar and Badharwa. The second storey is over the steps of the 14,000 ft high Pir Panjal range. The room inside is the Valley of Kashmir. The second storey is in the foothills of the Himalayas and shelters Ladakh and Baltistan. In the back yard is Gilgat.

The arteries of communication have brought Kashmir into contact with the world by means of roads which are not easily passable and meandering through difficult passes over colossal mountains.

A. Outlets Through the Pir Panjal Mountain Range.

Banihal Pass. The Banihal tunnel through the 8,200 ft pass, constructed with the aid of German technology, has made this road passable through winter as well. It links the Valley with Jammu and the upper Chinab and Punjab hills. There is an eerie curse on this link road. People have died every year traversing this mountain track. Trucks and buses wander into the 'Bloody Gorge' or 'Khuni Nala' and get killed. This year alone over 250 people lost their lives on this road. Unfortunately this is the only means of exit from the Valley of Kashmir into Jammu and India.

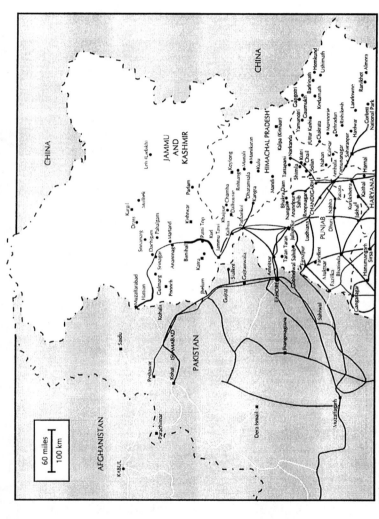

This map shows the only operational highway into Kashmir. The part shown as a thick line depicts the 'Devil's Precipice' where landslides and avalanches kill people every year. The road from Uri to Muzafarabad was the established artery of communication until 1947 – it is now occupied by the armies of India and Pakistan.

Budil Pass. This is a short cut from the Valley to Akhnoor over the other side of the Pir Panjal range. It is a pedestrian track through difficult terrain.

Rupri Pass. This traverses over 13000 feet north-west direct to Rajori. A pedestrian route used by pilgrims to Nandan Sar.

Mogul Road. This road was used by the Mogul emperors, and traverses the Pir Panjal range through Kousarnag, crossing the Rajori-Poonch road. On this road near Thana Mandi is the shrine of the saint Shahdara Sherif. Thana Mandi is famous for wood craftsmen. The road has 'sarias', camping motels for travelling monarchs, and links Poshiana to Aliabad. The story has it that in one Saria at Chingas, emperor Jahangir died. His wife Nur Jehan kept it a secret. She waited for rigor mortis to set in and dressed up the stiff body in king's clothes, and carried him in a palanquin to Lahore. This road has a potential to be developed if the two parts of Kashmir were reunited.

High passes are used by nomad shepherds to cross over through Sang-E-Safed, Noorpur, Chorgali and most important of all the Tosh Maidan pass. The later route was used in the old days by Pathan tribesmen from Lohara. The Loharian culture was a close variant of the Kashmiri way of life.

B. *Jhelum Gorge.*

This would have been the most sensible direct highway to the outside world. It runs along the Jhelum river and links Baramulla with Muzafarabad, now in the Pakistan side of Kashmir. The British had already prepared a plan for a rail link through this route into Kashmir. It was the ominous invasion of the Afghans which established this road. This was the shortest way into Peshawar through Hazier.

Hag Ir Pass. This road can be traversed to reach Ponch from Baramulla through Ir and the Ir Hag pass which is just over 8,652 feet. This is passable through winter.

C. *Passes Through the Northern Mountains.*

The mighty Karakoram range spans across 250 miles or 400 km, linked to the Himalayan peaks at its south and south-east limits. The Pamirs to the north-west and Kunlun Shan range to the east form a 'mountain knot' known as the 'roof of the world'. Its magnificent thirty-three peaks reach to a height of 23,950 ft above sea level. K2 is the second in from the eastern limit. One of the longest glaciers of the world known as Hispur is nestled in this range.

The passes through the north of Kashmir are formidable. The access into Chilas, then Yasin and Chitral has to cross the Karakoram Highway. The Kishan Ganga territory of Karnah and Gurez leads into the mountains, the Mintaka pass into Wakhan Afghanistan, the Khunjerab pass into the foothills of the Pamirs. The Karakoram mountain range has passes like Shimshal Pass and Karakoram Pass linking Ladakh with Sinkiang, China. The area occupied by China is Aksai Chin through which a Chinese road is currently in use, and is accessed through Changchenmo route, a hilly track from Ladakh.

The Zojila Pass starts at the junction of Haramukh and the Nanga Parbat mountains through 11,300 peaks into Baltistan and Ladakh, and then on to Tibet and Mongolia.

D.   *The Road From the Eastern Mountains of Kashmir to Kishtawar.*

This road could be developed through the Marbal Pass and link Kishtawar with the Valley.

The Srinager to Kashgar road brought cashmere wool for shawl makers in Kashmir. Unfortunately it also brought the Chinese army into Aksai Chin, Kashmiri territory now occupied by the Chinese since 1962.

The premise that Kashmir is landlocked can be refuted on the basis of the numerous outlets to surrounding countries. The big question is to find a friendly country which will allow access to the outside world.

1. Kashmir can demand access routes in international forums governed by laws on international access routes and air corridors.

2. Kashmir has rivers of great importance which are the lifeline for agriculture in both India and Pakistan, and for hydroelectric and irrigation projects like the Mangla Dam in Pakistan. It will be possible to have bilateral agreements where water from Kashmir can be traded for the import of merchandise. Forest products, fruit and handicrafts from Kashmir are commodities which can be bartered for

salt, sugar and fuel. The network of roads still extant will need upgrading and could be put into instant use.

3. Tourism in India and Pakistan will flourish if roads into Kashmir are open and serviceable. Millions of tourists from all over the world visiting Kashmir, albeit 'peaceful Kashmir', will have stop-over breaks in India and Pakistan.

4. All roads open and soft borders established, free flow of people travelling can be achieved.

Kashmir in a way is landlocked now. Progress, and prosperity are at a standstill. Industries have failed to thrive except in Jammu, which has kept up with the pace of development because of road and railway links. One by one all industries in Kashmir have disappeared. The present road out of Kashmir is inadequate for trade and very risky for passenger traffic. Every year more people die and more trucks and coaches fall into the gorge or get buried under a landslide.

Ladakh

The Ladakh province of Kashmir has two important districts, Leh and Kargil. Leh is mainly Buddhist and Kargil Shia Muslim. The population of 140,000 is spread throughout the enormous expanse of the region.

Kushuk Bakula, the Head Lama, was a member of the Kashmiri constituent assembly. He made it clear that he did not like the land reforms and rule from Srinager was unpalatable to him. He did not like the Chinese either. He was between the devil of the land reform and the deep blue sea of Communist rule. He started looking at possible autonomy with special relations with India. Tibet would be the last resort. The people of Kargil will not go along with these plans.

The people of Ladakh have strong traditions extant. The Indian army have lived in the place since 1947. Tourism and trade brought a new civilisation to the region. The established values of the most ancient race in the world were being defiled. Sonam Gyalsan, a lawyer from Ladakh, felt the change was telling on the people. "We tribespeople are the modern day untouchables of Kashmir," he pronounced in desperation. Leh has an airport which is considered to be an engineering miracle, in view of the terrain. Chandigarh in India is now connected directly to Ladakh by an air corridor.

The population of Ladakh has been on the decline over the years. The birth rate, in spite of better medical facilities, is declining. The reasons can be summarised.

(a) Ladakh along with Siberia is the coldest inhabited place on the face of the earth. The fertility in men could be affected.

(b) The ratio of women to men is 1:4. The Buddhist community of Ladakh are normally private and reserved. The story, however, does go round that three brothers would have to share one wife! A slipper outside the bedroom door would identify which of the brothers was inside. The tale may only be conjecture. Ladakhi people have made tremendous advances in education. This practice must be waning now.

(c) Most of the men dedicated to the monastery are celibate and dedicate their lives to the monastery and religion, and these Lamas become teachers, physicians, astrologers, landlords and magistrates. They would not get married. They are timid and hibernate during the winter months. In some rare instances one family may be a mixture of Muslim and Buddhist religions. They cook Halal meat but still drink the strong alcohol 'Chaang'. Ladakh is dependent on every means of livelihood like food and clothing from outside. Ladakh for hundreds of years was liable to the Tibet ecclesiastical fealty tribute in the form of salt, and paid them taxes. The Chinese claim that Ladakh was a part of Tibet.

The plateau of Aksai Chin links the industrial province of Sinkiang with Tibet. If the Chinese lose Sinkiang they lose Tibet and inner Mongolia. Aksai Chin is the traffic artery to western Tibet and Sinkiang. This is the reason why the Ching dynasty of 18th Century ancient China had check posts on this route. Ladakh itself has the best access from Srinager and therefore will benefit most from being a part of the state.

Jammu

Travelling through the Banihall tunnel from Kashmir on a bleak and cold winter's day you emerge at the other end with clear blue sky and warm air greeting you. The transformation in the weather is sensational within minutes of the journey. The tunnel penetrates the Pir Panjal mountains, and as if in defiance of being violated the mountain range still takes lives every year either by landslides or avalanches. This road meanders through steep sharp bends all the way to the winter capital Jammu. Jammu is 290 km from Srinager.

Jammu is a city of spires standing proud in the skyline from Hindu temples all over. The most famous of all is the Rughunath temple built by Gulab Singh in 1835. The other outstanding features are the Amar Mahal Palace (now used as a museum), and Bahu fort with the temple of Kali Goddess inside. The city itself is on hills converging towards the Tawi river. The river originates from the Chinani hills and bisects the city into old and new parts before merging, with the Chinab river. The tropical comforting feeling starts as you reach Udhampur, a busy town from where you can proceed to Jammu city or the Ramnagar and Poonch/Rajori areas on the Pakistan side of the rest of Kashmir. Jammu offers the route to Zanskar through Pedar Valley, famous for its sapphire mines. This part of the province, about 180 km north of Jammu, has beautiful places like Buderwah and Kishtawar. Buderwah (also called Little Kashmir) has tall snow-peaked mountains like the Kailas, overlooking beautiful lakes like the Kund. The Kishtawar to Zanskar stretch is used by trekkers for a lifetime experience of climbing. Kishtawar can also be reached from Kashmir direct, through Kokernag and Daksum across the Simthan road. Jammu has a railway line which connects it to the Indian railway network.

The geopolitical orientation of the territories of Kashmir has a strong bearing on the causes of its troubles and reasons why solutions are stymied. The region is a buffer between violent nations, a wall to peep over the neighbours, a springboard for a dive into the domain of the other superpower, an arena for a bout of boxing, a crunchy meal for a nibble, and not least a beautiful paradise with a wealth of nature's attributes and good-looking people – docile, altruistic and governable. It is these same people who have now woken up to realities of life and they want to live with peace, in their own home.

HISTORY OF KASHMIR

Rocky Milestones in the History of Kashmir

'A glorious people vibrated again the lightening of the nations'

(Shelley)

People of Kashmir want to live in their own den away from the tribulations inflicted on them by the cruel outside world. They have a long history of suffering behind them. The landmarks of interminable despotic rule and events wrapped round the destiny of the people, had a profound effect on the culmination of the present society in Kashmir.

As far back as the first written words of history, Kashmir has been at the receiving end of invasions by foreigners. Pandavas, Maurya, Kushan (Mongolian nomads), Gonandya, Karkota, Utpala and Lohara at various stages swooped in and created havoc. The invaders descended from Tibet, Russia, Mongolia, Afghanistan, China and India. Kashmir, with its docile people and thirty-two passes through the mountains was a soft target. It was foray and plunder at first, then they stayed on to extract more and rule as despots. For King Nero, who had the city of Rome burnt, the sight of flames would stimulate his mind to write poetry. Most invaders enjoyed torturing the natives and destroying their habitats. The cadence of Nero's verses would have spoken of the agony and devastation which he himself created in the first place. The looters of Kashmir revelled in the anguish they caused, just for the sake of being capable of doing so.

The tyrannical monarchs such as Mihira Kula, The White Hun, or Shankaravarman left lasting impressions on the people.

The Jhelum river and the Hydaspes formed the eastern limit for the advances of Alexander the Great of Macedonia. He left behind a big contingent of his army. Formal Ancient Greek architecture can be seen in monuments and ancient buildings.

Kashmir is where three great powers, Russia, China and South Asia meet; three languages, Dardic Kashmiri, Tibeto-Chinese and Anglo-British blend, and three religions, Buddhism, Hinduism and Islam harmonise. Buddhism was the universal faith during Ashoka rule. Hinduism was introduced by the Brahmin priests and Hindu rulers. Islam was introduced by the mystic saints and preachers from Iran.

Kashmir was annexed as an appendage to greater China by Kanishka all through the second century.

Third Century BC Ashoka the Bhuddist king made Srinagar the capital of his huge empire. The Bhuddists ruled Kashmir up to the eighth century AD and left their culture and monasteries, especially in Ladakh; the whole of Kashmir is proud of this. Ashoka was a powerful ruler and Kashmir was his base.

Huns gained control of the Valley in the early sixth century. Mihira Kula was one of the Hun princes known as 'Cruel as death' for his ruthless behaviour.

AD 530 the Ujjain empire took control of the administering of Kashmir. Ujjain kings had control until *697* when the local Hindu Brahman rule was established.

724-761 The Hindu king Lalityaditya, marked an era of literature and learning. In his time Punjab was conquered and annexed to Kashmir. He led his armies deep into South India and the Turkistan-Tibet regions. The king was keen on filling his coffers, and then passing the burden of his objectives onto his subjects. He constructed temples at Avantipora and Martand. The one in Martand was based on the Hindu God – Shiva. The stone Lingam is partly submerged in Lake Mansbal. The temple at Pandrethan is occupied by the army now. He set an example for an independent country, 'Kashmir', making other states subservient.

In 855 Avantivarman, Lalityaditya's son was generous and parted with the ill-gotten treasures of his father. His civil engineer Suyya built waterways and embankments along Jhelum and Sindh. He was rewarded by making a town for himself. He built the town along the river he had tamed, called after him, Suyyapore. (Now known as Sopore or Little London, for its prosperity from apple orchards.)

It was during the inauspicious period *(939-944)* that King Unmattavati ruled and administered torture by the use of arm splitting, by the throwing of daggers which plunged into the hollows between the breasts of naked women. He then ripped the abdomens of the pregnant women apart to see their foetuses. This atrocity was later replicated by the Dogra rulers as if to emulate the despotic rule.

The saga of repression continued as the throne was passed down.

1089-1101 King Harisha ruled with greed and extravagance as his hallmark. The taxes became intolerable. A reign of terror and repression followed and went on until his demise.

The Hindu rule was dominated by Lalityaditya. The written works on Kashmir emanate from this period. Pundit Kalhane the great poet of twelfth century wrote *Rajatarangin* (River of Kings). These essays were the first ever work recorded from Kashmir and in 1148 were translated into Persian on orders from Akbar, the Mogul king of India. "Kashmir may be conquered by force of spiritual merit but never by force of soldiers", an extract from *Rajatarangin,* is worth remembering in the present political climate.

The spate of relative tranquillity was short-lived and the dreaded invasion from Mongolia was heralded. Ferocious Tartars from Mongolia *(1300-1320)* marauded Kashmir. Zulfi Khan from the Chengiz Khan family whirlwinded into Kashmir. He was called the 'Dulchi' and he ruthlessly indulged in looting and arson. He took fifty thousand slaves with him, when he decided to cart the loot back to Mongolia. He perished in a blizzard crossing the Devasar pass along with all the wealth and people he carried with him. Kashmir was left in an abyss of devastation.

Simha Deva, the ruler defeated by the Tartars found his way back from Kishtawar with his commander in chief Ram Chand. He knew Zulfi Khan had perished and the throne was there to take. Ram Chand, a Kashmiri by birth, wanted the throne for himself. He met Rinchen, the visiting Tibetan prince, and sought his help. Rinchen killed him instead and married his daughter Kuta Rani. That way he got both the throne and his beautiful daughter. Rinchen was readily accepted as the ruler. It was around *1320* when he came to Kashmir to seek wealth. Kashmir, having experienced devastation from the Tartars, made him a popular king, hoping for the lesser evil. Rinchen took Shah Mir, a Muslim from Swat, into his service as his chief adviser. Rinchen converted to Islam, after having observed Bulbul Shah, a popular Sufi saint in his prayers and impressed by his devotion to the faith. He called himself Sultan Sadr-ud-din and built the Jama Masjid and Ziyarat Bulbul Shah in his short two and a half years' rule. Bulbul Shah introduced Sufism, an ideology 'free from greed and abstinence from all instinctual desires'. His lifestyle and devotion lured people to Sufism and Islam.

The yearning for revenge was seething in the background and when Rinchen died, Simbha Deva's brother, Udayadeva, came back from hiding and married Kuta Rani. Kuta Rani fought wars for him and ruled Kashmir for fifty days, after which Shah Mir, who was waiting in the wings, took over the throne. This marked the start of the Sultan dynasty that lasted for two hundred years. It was still not a bed of roses for Kashmiris – as we shall see.

Shah Hamadan, Mir Syed Ali arrived from Iran with thousands of followers in *1372*, and with him came designs for carpets, woollen garments, copper utensils and papier maché. He spread the message of Islam and converted masses of people to his faith. This was a golden era for Kashmir. A renascence of culture, understanding and tolerance was heralded. It was soon after in *1377* that another great saint, Sheikh Nur-ud-Din Wali, dominated the lives of Hindus and Muslims alike. Chrar Sherif Shrine, his resting place, is very popular for pilgrimages and has been so ever since that time. Recently, on May 11th, 1995, the Indian army laid a siege on the shrine in order to capture militants. They ultimately burnt down the shrine with adjacent mosque and 2500 homes.

It was Shah Mir who was the founder of the Sultan dynasty. His rule was followed by Sultan Skinder *(1389-1413)*. The sultan built the Khanqah Moula Shrine, known to be the resting place of Mir Syed Ali Hamadani, and visited by worshippers of both Islamic and Hindu faiths. Also known as *Butshikan*, or iconoclast, he destroyed the idols used by Hindu worshippers after they converted to Islam. He burnt seven maunds (500 lb) of sacred thread from converted Hindus (the thread is a cotton string worn round the body for life).

The golden era in the history of Kashmir was heralded when Zain ul Abiddin inherited the throne from his father, Sultan Skinder in *1420* – and ruled for fifty years. Also known as The Great King (Budshah), his rule has been remarkable in progress, prosperity and justice. He invited artists from Iran, and the handicraft industry for which Kashmir prides itself was born. The exquisite papier maché, wood carving and carpet weaving crafts were started. Budshah rule extended from Kashmir to Tibet and Punjab. He was responsible for the construction of Zaina Kadal (Fourth Bridge) and the Zain Lank, the man-made island in Lake Wular. He built a palace on the island which was a symbol for peace and tranquillity, an ultimate retreat. The inscription on the stone slab forming the facade of the palace said in Persian, 'May this edifice be as firm as the foundations of the heavens. As long as the monarch, Zain ul Abiddin, holds festivals herein, may it be like the date of his own reign, happy.' This stone has disappeared. He built the Zaina Dab, a magnificent building with twelve storeys, each storey containing fifty rooms with each room big enough to take five hundred people. Chaks, a tribe from Dardistan, set fire to the building in an attempt to undermine his rule. He married two daughters of a Hindu Raja of Jammu. Budshah died in 1470 and his majestic tomb stands today near the Fourth Bridge in Srinagar, Kashmir. All my own family who have passed away are buried here.

It was ominous for Shah Mir's family that he passed away, because the children, Mohammed Shah and Fath Shah, fell out and fought for the throne all through the period *1484-1511*. Their rule came to an end and the Chak family, waiting in the wings, found their way into the realms of power and ruled Kashmir from *1555 to 1586*. A short but eventful period of history ensued. The Chaks were Shiis Muslims and established their rule against their rivals Megris and Rainas. The period of rule under Yousuf Shah Chak was the most outstanding. The communities of Kashmir were united and the country was thriving. The wife of the ruler, Haba Khatoon, is the greatest poet Kashmir has ever known and she was a great philosopher. The Haba Khatoon mountain range is named after her, and her folk songs have kept her alive forever in the minds of

Kashmiris. She advised her husband against accepting the invitation from the Indian Mogul King, Akbar, to visit India. Had he followed this advice, he would not have been arrested perfidiously and Kashmir would not have been a part of the Indian Mogul empire for the next 166 years! He languished in Akbar's jail and died there. He is buried near Patna Bihar and his anniversary is celebrated. Yaqub Khan Chak and Shamsi Chak helped to ward off the first two of Akbar's attacks. This was the first time that Kashmir would be ruled from India. The first few attempts to capture Kashmir having failed, Akbar sent forty thousand horsemen and twenty thousand foot soldiers under the command of Mirza Kasim, who captured Kashmir on *June 5th, 1586.* Akbar entered Kashmir preceded by five thousand labourers to clear the way from Lahore to Srinagar. The journey took six weeks.

The long Mogul era in Kashmir, *1586-1752,* was now heralded. Moguls gave to Kashmir as well as taking from it. They left it more beautiful than they found it. They were civilised and had a taste for natural beauty. Kashmir was nevertheless ruled from India and the people of Kashmir were still a nonentity. Akbar even chose to humiliate them by dressing men as females in long robes. The idea was to kill the male instinct in them, so that they would not fight against his rule.

Nur-ud-Din Jahangir inherited the throne after Akbar and played an important role in building the image of Kashmir as the Shangri-La of the East. He and his wife, Nur Jehan, built the famous Mogul gardens and planted the chinar trees, the national tree of Kashmir. Jahangir became obsessed with Kashmir. He was on his way back to India, travelling from Kashmir, when he stopped for the night in a saria (rest house) at Baramgala, Kashmir. He died here, but his wife dressed him like the King and sat him on a palanquin for the continuing journey. She declared him dead when the party arrived back. This was in the year *1627.* During his last breath of life, he uttered, 'Kashmir only Kashmir', and died. He built 777 gardens around Lake Dal. His mother-in-law extracted scented essence from rose petals. The revenue from this 'Atter' was enormous. Nur Jehan his wife, in her sixteen years of marriage to him, had made her own gardens in Kashmir. Daragha Bagh on Lake Mansbal was one of them and Pather Masjid in the city of Srinagar had gardens and a mosque made from grey stones, which are still standing.

Shah Jehan stepped in after Jahangir and built Chashma Shahi. The beautifully carved marble basin housing the 'spring' has since been stolen and replaced by a makeshift concrete tank. In the year *1640*, Shah Jehan's son, Murad, married a Kashmiri girl and like his parents, loved Kashmir. He built the island Char Chinar (Sona Lank); only photographs can relive the beauty of the man-made island, which is almost desecrated now.

Dara Shikoh, the eldest son of Shah Jehan, built a place for spiritual learning for his guide Akhund Mulla Shah on the top of the hill overlooking Lake Dal. The structure is partly preserved and is called the 'Pari Mahal' (Palace of Fairies). He also built the grey stone mosque near Makhdoom Sahib, now in ruins, and the stone bridge in Bijbehara with gardens on either side. He was ambitious but lost the throne to his brother, Aurangzeb, who beheaded him. Aurangzeb was a strict Muslim who wanted to govern on the tenets of Islam.

December 1664: Aurangzeb, along with his sister Roshan Ara Begam, set off for Kashmir. The whole court from Delhi set off on a grand procession, including 100,000 horsemen, camels, elephants, oxen, and cattle. Elephants fell down the precipice of the Pir Panjal range, from a hazardous road which was only designed for mules. He had chosen the wrong time of year to travel. The Mogul dynasty was getting feeble and was in disarray. Aurangzeb's successors plunged the country of Kashmir into strife and anarchy. The most inspiring era of architectural excellence and powerful rule came to a sad end.

The effects of the invasion of India by the Persian leader Nadir Shah in *1739* were felt in Kashmir. He shook India with the ferocity of his invasion, killed 30,000 men, took the peacock throne and Kohinoor, the most precious jewel in the world. He left the broken up remains of the Mogul empire in disarray. The administration of the whole kingdom collapsed, inviting predators from the region. It was not long after that, that the Afghans invaded Kashmir and defeated the last of the Moguls. The Afghan rule lasted from *1752 to 1809* and they left memories of reprobate atrocities for people of Kashmir to contend with. Ahmad Shah Abdali ruled to despoil the little possessions people had. He was very ruthless and cruel towards Kashmiris. He would order members of the public, who were not to his liking, to be executed or to be drowned in Lake Dal.

The Afghans built the first bridge (Amira Kadal) over the Jhelum, and the old Palace 'Shergari' on the bank of the river. One Afghan governor, Atta Mohammed Khan, built the Hari Parbat Fort. His name is inscribed on the fifth gate of the fort. The eighteen year old Azad Khan was the worst of all Afghans governors. He plundered, killed, and raped like a lunatic. He slit the stomach of his doctor for not curing an eye ailment he was suffering from.

The eventful Afghan rule came to an end in *1818* when Abdali (Durani) died in Kabul. His governor in Kashmir rushed back to grab the throne and took with him most of the army. An opening was created in Kashmir for a soft landing. It was at the behest of some Kashmiris that Sikhs from Punjab walked into defenceless Kashmir. The hope was that a better administration would be put into place. The worst fears were realised as the new rulers became entrenched. It was like coming out of the frying pan into the fire.

The Sikhs ruled Kashmir from *1819* for twenty-seven long years, right up to the time they were defeated by the British in *1846*. The Sikh governors treated the people in Kashmir as little better than cattle. The murder of a native by a Sikh was punishable by a fine of sixteen to twenty rupees, of which four rupees were paid to the family of the victim if he was a Hindu and two rupees if he was a Muslim. Muslims were hanged or stoned to death if they slaughtered a cow for meat (once a family of seventeen were burnt alive for killing a cow). All mosques were closed. The farmers were taxed to give nine tenths of the crop. As if the suffering from this despotic rule was not enough, people also faced the worst epidemics of cholera, devastating earthquakes, followed by the famine of 1832, due to floods. The population was decimated with combined effects of evil rule and natural calamity. People died like flies in a storm. The population was reduced from 800,000 to less than 200,000. Ranjit Singh, the Sikh ruler from Punjab, never came to Kashmir and distanced himself from the problems facing the country. He did however want all the taxes he could get, the pashmina shawls and the women from Kashmir. On his death his four wives and five Kashmiri slave girls were flung on his burning funeral pyre. Ranjit Singh employed Gulab Singh, a Dogra army officer, for a salary of three rupees per month. Gulab Singh won the favour of his master by faithful services rendered during the capture of Kashmir and the war with the British.

He was rewarded with Jammu as his Jaghir (a sort of freehold ownership of property). He became the autocratic ruler of Jammu in 1830. He consolidated power and conquered Ladakh from Tibet and Dardistan (little Tibet) in 1840. In the meantime, Poonch was taken over by Dyan Singh, the brother of Gulab Singh and the state began to take shape.

The British took control of Kashmir from the chaotic regime of Sikhs, using the help of Gulab Singh, who forgot the favour the Sikhs had done to him making him the ruler of Jammu! He fought against his old master and on *March 16th, 1846* he helped the British to win the second Sikh war. The British imposed a heavy fine on the Sikhs which they could not pay. They offered Jammu and Kashmir instead. It was Gulab Singh who interceded and paid the fine. Kashmir was sold to Gulab Singh and the sale deed was conducted through the Treaty of Amritsar. Sir Harding, the incumbent Governor General, sold Kashmir to Gulab Singh for a sum of 750,000 rupees, one horse, twelve goats (six male and six female) and three shawls. One shawl and one hundred goats also had to be given every year otherwise Kashmir would revert back and be surrendered to the British: the British supremacy would still remain. Gilgat was included in the treaty but Gulab Singh could not control the defiant natives and the British, for fear of a Russian invasion over the Pamirs, established the Gilgat Agency and direct rule. Gulab Singh marched into Kashmir to claim his commodity, purchased at a bargain price. He was pushed back and chased by the local people. Promptly, through the services of Henry Lawrence, he obtained help from the British army and got himself installed in power on *November 19th, 1846*. Almost exactly one hundred years later, it was again the British who helped to bring an end to Dogra rule, as a last fling before their own exit from the subcontinent.

Gulab Singh conquered Dardistan and annexed it to the state. Now Gulab Singh had annexed all territories together, to make Jammu and Kashmir a whole country for the first time.

The life of a Kashmiri remained a saga of poverty and repression, and the Muslims remained the victims of vengeance sought against five hundred years of Muslim rule. They still went to the gallows for killing a cow and were used as forced labour (Beggar System): "The majority had to submit to religious prejudices of a small minority,"

(E.F. Knight, 1850). Gulab Singh wanted to convert all Muslims to Hinduism by force, but the high priests of Banaras, now Varanasi – the sacred city of Hindus in India, demurring his wild plans, refused to give their blessing.

India was going through a dynamic political change. The Muslims and high caste Hindus in the Bengal army accused their British officers of intentionally subverting their faith. This mutiny in 1856 resulted in religion playing an important role in the politics of India. Kashmir felt the ripples of these waves striking at its grass roots. There was subversion and despotic rule pointed at the Muslim population.

In *1857* Gulab Singh was succeeded by Rambir Singh. He was described as a noble ruler but still the head of a repressive regime. Rambir Singh helped the British retake Delhi after a mutiny. In 1860 Robert Thorp, born to a Kashmiri mother, exposed Rambir Singh's atrocities in the Indian papers. He was murdered for that worthy cause. His grave is in the Srinagar cemetery.

The Great Famine of *1870* was caused by floods inundating all the crops. Thousands died from starvation and a mass exodus took place. Kashmiris migrated in thousands to parts of India and Africa. Thousands were flayed at the border for escaping.

Families who escaped from Kashmir are living with strident memories of forced migration by their elders and have therefore maintained an identity of their root culture.

Kashmir has been a soft target for all invaders. In *1878* the Russian invasion of Kashmir was hatched. The Soviet generals, Peroski, Duhamel and Khrular made plans to invade Kashmir through Chitral. They would have taken India in their fold. They had the approval of Tsar Nicholas, but it did not materialise because of the British presence in the area.

In the meantime, the Dogra dynasty was digging its heels deeper into the core of Kashmir society and maintained its rule. Rambir Singh passed away and was succeeded by Major General Pratap Singh in 1885. His rule lasted for a brief period only, but fortuitously allowed the British resident to be installed in Kashmir for the first time. The British now got involved with the administration, and Mr

Walter Lawrence was appointed as a revenue commissioner. He was responsible for restoring land tenants' rights and had the forced free labour 'beggar' abolished.

Sixteen years of direct rule by the British government followed, beginning in 1889.

This short spell of relief from Dogra rule gave a breathing space for the people and reforms were executed. Pratap Singh had no son and the British were concerned about the activities of the Russians on the Pamirs, so they put more army on the border and took control in their own hands. This was a period of some respite for people and reforms were introduced to alleviate the suffering of the people. In November, 1890, the Kohala-Srinagar road was completed. The main artery of communication between Kashmir and the rest of the world was constructed by Mr Spedding, a British civil engineer. It was the finest mountain road in the world at that time and a lifeline for Kashmir. A plan was prepared by British engineers to make a railway track along that route.

Unfortunately for the Kashmiris, the Maharaja was reinstalled in 1905 and the saga of despotic rule continued.

Pratap Singh (not having his own son) relinquished the throne reluctantly to his westernised nephew, Hari Singh. Hari Singh, son of Amar Singh, the younger brother of Pratap Singh, was born in France and educated there. On a state visit to England he was received by King George and Queen Mary. He carried on with his autocratic rule of Kashmir with the help of the British. He played polo and liked fishing. His western hobbies helped to instil some life into the administration by developing facilities for tourism.

The British were actively helping to transform Kashmir and installed many outstanding institutions. Kashmir carpets were exhibited in the Chicago World Fair for the first time. The 'Bund' in Srinagar, the shopping parade along the Jhelum, Peston Ji and his 'white horse' statue for whisky, Lloyds Bank, the Post Office, Nedu's Hotel, Missionary hospitals in Drugjan Baramula and Anantnag were some of the outstanding projects started by the British.

Dr Arthur Neve, a missionary surgeon, performed twenty major operations a day! The Mission School was established and Cecil

Tyndale Biscoe had a difficult time in getting Muslim boys to begin school. He created a revolution in the education of children in Kashmir. The Kangri-clutching, lazy and arrogant boys became pupils, eager to learn and become educated. These people are the adults of today. He and Blanche Biscoe served Kashmir like no one else ever had. They retired and were given a good send-off in 1947, after fifty-seven years of wonderful service which infused confidence and a sense of self-esteem into Kashmiri Education. This was the beginning of politics in Kashmir, and in 1924 an important event in its political history took place. It was the Srinagar Silk Weaving factory workers' strike. The labour force came out in defiance of strict rules for the first time against wages and working conditions. They occupied government land forcibly. The leaders of the strike were punished. Mr Said-ud-Din Shawl was expelled from service and the little holding (Jagir), belonging to Noor Shah Naqshband, was withdrawn from him. The two leaders, accompanied by the religious leader, Mirwaiz of Jamia Masjid, submitted a memo to Lord Reading, the incumbent viceroy, listing their grievances to forestall violence. This marked the beginning of the uprising against Maharaja Hari Singh.

The virus of 'freedom' caught on and spread. People realised that the injustice of being ruled like slaves must be challenged. They worked hard for a living and were still left spiritless and easily awed, as the Dogras pushed them to the limits of abject poverty. They were subject to excessive taxation to satisfy the rapacity of the Maharaja. Forced labour and oppressive laws were still in force. Shanker Lal Kaul, a Hindu activist, started 'Kashmiricus' (Kashmir for the Kashmiris) movement. The State Subject Law was introduced as a result of these pressure groups.

People of Kashmir owe gratitude to the services of Sir Tyndale Biscoe and Miss Melinson, and Dr and Mrs Edmunds in the missionary schools who laid the foundations of real education in Kashmir. The first bicycle was introduced by Tyndale Biscoe. It was a spectacular novelty and frightfully exciting. The infrastructure was laid for many thousands of people to receive education. Hospitals, likewise, were started by missionary medical staff, mainly from England. It was his work in Kashmir which provided research material for Dr Nevelle thus enabling him to report Kangri cancer to the world. Burns suffered due to a chronic exposure to heat, as a cause of cancer, was first reported from Kashmir. The skin of the abdomen becomes first discoloured and then ulcerated to result in cancer. Prolonged exposure to burning coal in earthen pots next to bare skin, in order to keep warm, caused the burns.

July 13th, 1931, was an important day. Reports reached Srinagar that a Hindu policeman had desecrated Quran to intimidate the Kashmiri prisoners in a Jammu prison. This sparked off violent protest marches. Nine people were gunned down by the state army in front of the Central jail in Srinagar. This day is the Martyrs' Day remembered every year. This action resulted in the setting up of the Glancy Commission to investigate injustices of the Maharaja's administration.

The first political party ever to be formed in Kashmir was started by Mr Sheikh Mohammed Abdullah this time in 1931. A school teacher, he took the plight of Kashmiris to heart. His mandate was 'democracy and justice'. He named the party, 'Muslim Conference'. The ruler did not like this. Several thousand people were killed in the agitation which followed and the army was in the streets with orders to kill at sight anyone leading the demonstrations. The Dogra bullets claimed their first casualties in the streets of Kashmir. The British government in Delhi sent in the Glancy Commission to investigate the atrocities of the Dogra army. The Dogra ruler had organised the brutality, spearheaded by the minions of law and order.

The 'Muslim Conference' of Abdullah was changed to the 'National Conference' in order to give it a secular shape and incorporate Hindus and Sikhs in the revolt against the despotic ruler. The NC party got an instant approval by the Indian congress with nationalistic ideals. In Jammu, however, the 'Muslim Conference' kept its name under the leadership of Choudry Gulam Abbas. The revolt against the Maharaja intensified and in 1933 there was open support from the Punjab Muslim Ahrar Party. They sent help into Kashmir. In the following year, there was a call for civil disobedience from Choudry Gulam Abbas. The Maharaja caved in and passed The Constituent Assembly Act. Thirty-five of the seventy seats of the assembly would be nominated and the rest elected by an election. The Muslim conference got fourteen seats.

In India the British by this time showed the first signs of giving in to pressure for the 'freedom struggle' by the Indians. The Government of India Act of 1935 came into force. Indians were offered full control of the administration of India, except in defence and foreign affairs. India would become a federal state, including in its fold all five hundred states who were invited by the viceroy to join the Federation. As expected, they all refused.

The spirit of Democracy was getting hold of the people in Kashmir. The first ever newspaper, *Hamdard*, was launched by Mr Prem Nath Bazaz and Sheikh Abdullah. The paper became the voice of revolution against the autocratic rule of Hari Singh. The pressures were mounting on the Maharaja and a gradual relaxation of repressive laws became necessary. In 1939 the Jammu and Kashmir Constitution Act no 14, was passed. A council of ministers had control over juridical and legislative matters. The two capitals, Srinagar and Jammu were administered by municipal corporations, four-fifths of which were elected. The smaller places were administered through Town Area Committees. Limited powers were given to small local councils and the practice was continued through this, so-called, local democratic rule. 5000 villages were fused into 720 districts, but the main power was with the district commissioners and the ruler. Sir Albion Benerji resigned as prime minister because he felt strongly about the injustices Muslims were suffering. He said, "all Muslims are illiterate, steeped in poverty and driven like dumb cattle."

The first national conference meeting of Mr Abdullah took place in Baramulla on September 29th, 1940. Sardar Budh Singh was elected as the president. Nationalistic slogans were reiterated and unity against the Maharaja's rule was the focus of the meeting.

The introduction of politics into their lives did not change much for the people and despite the reforms, the plight of Kashmiris remained a saga of poverty and slave labour. Every commodity was heavily taxed. 93.4% of the total population were illiterate (1941) and net annual income was Rs 74 (£1.50) per family for those who had some land. In 1945 the per capita income for landless people was only Rs 11 and out of this sum they had to pay Rs 1 per head in taxes. One family had to sustain life with Rs 50 per head for the year. This was the extent of poverty only two years before independence.

Mr Abdullah was active in his campaign as head of the National Conference Party, running it from his reading room office. He published a document called 'New Kashmir' in early 1944. The hallmark of the campaign was the red flag with a plough in the middle. The constitution of the party contained a charter for the peasant and a 'land to tiller' policy was adopted. The charter also declared equal rights to women and all classes of people. A year later, in July of 1945, Sheikh Abdullah and his party demonstrated their allegiance to the Indian Congress. Pandit Nehru, Moulana Azad, Samad Khan Achakzai, Asif Ali from the Indian Congress were given a spectacular reception by Abdullah and his party when they came to Kashmir. Bakshi Gulam Mohammed organised a boat flotilla of thousands of shikaras decorated to form a reverie procession. Each side of the River Jhelum was decorated with flags and ornate posters. The river's banks were filled with people. An ostentatious spectacle, this action proved fatal for the future history of Kashmir. The Indian camp were convinced that the people of Kashmir were for India and made up Nehru's mind to take the steps he later took as prime minister of India.

Independence for India was imminent and the British cabinet mission met in Delhi to discuss the future of the princely states in late 1946. It was the first error of judgement on Mr Abdullah's part not to send his representative. Mirza Afzal Beg was a minister in the Maharaja's Cabinet. He was asked to resign by Abdullah in order not to be a part of the negotiating team to meet the British mission. Mr Abdullah sent a memo to the mission, instead, saying, "We demand our basic democratic rights to enable us to send our selected representative to the constitution-making bodies that will construct the framework of free India. We emphatically repudiate the right of princely order to represent the people." The memo was ignored and a chance to make an impact on the commission about the plight of people was lost. It was in about March, 1946, that a prominent Kashmiri, Pandit Sir Tej Bahadur Sapru, Maharaja's legal adviser and an Urdu scholar, had the Urdu language recognised as the official language and he was instrumental in the appointment of Mirza Afzal Beg and Ganga Ram from Kashmir and Jammu respectively as ministers. On May 20th, 1946, the 'Quit Kashmir' movement was launched by Mr Abdullah, demanding the end of Dogra rule. He was put in prison for treason, followed by a wave of arrests of the national conference workers. Carnage followed: twenty people were killed and many hundreds injured by the army. A reign of terror was let loose. Respectable citizens were forced to dig up trenches and sweep the roads. In the prison, the two leaders, Choudry Gulam Abbas and Sheikh Abdullah conferred and decided to work together on a joint strategy to oust the autocratic ruler. That merger between the two never came about. An error was made again.

The Maharaja was spurred on by his prime minister to be firm and show defiance. On June 19th, 1946, Pandit Jawaharlal Nehru entered Kashmir in spite of a ban on his entry. Mr Nehru was concerned for the masses in Kashmir. He stated: "Srinagar has been transformed into a graveyard. I must go." He was arrested. His arrival in Kashmir was met with a black flag demonstration by some Pandits under the leadership of Shiv Narayan Fotedar. An esoteric gesture because it was only Muslim bodies which filled the graves! Three days later Nehru was released and flown back in a private plane sent by Percival Archibald Wavell, the viceroy of India.

1947 was the year of 'independence' for India. Mountbatten came on the scene, first as viceroy, then as Governor General of India. On *June 13th, 1947* he called a meeting of all party leaders. The issue of the princely states was discussed. Mr Nehru said that there was no trace in the cabinet mission memo of any state being allowed to claim independence. Mr Jinnah reiterated that "States are fully entitled to say if they will join neither dominion, and the cabinet mission has never laid down that every state was bound to come into one or the other constituent assembly." Four days later Mr Jinnah repeated in a statement, that "Constitutionally and legally the Indian states will be independent sovereign states on the termination of paramountcy and they will be free to decide for themselves and to adopt any course they like. They can decide to remain independent. In the last case they enter into agreements and relationships, such as economic or commercial, with Hindustan or Pakistan as they may choose."

The British viceroy, Lord Mountbatten was tossing territories and people in them in all directions, playing a key role in the division of India. He made a visit to Kashmir on June 19th, 1947, and stayed as a guest of the Maharaja in a fishing lodge, in order to persuade him to affiliate himself with India or Pakistan. He later spoke in a meeting of the East India Association in London. "I went personally and saw the

Maharaja of Kashmir. I spent four days with him. On every one of these days I persisted with the same advice. Ascertain the will of the people by any means and join whichever dominion your people wish to join by August 14th of this year. He did not do that. What happened can be seen. Had he acceded to Pakistan I had assurance from the government of India that no objection will be raised. Had he acceded to India, Pakistan did not exist at that time and would not have interfered."

Hari Singh, an old time polo mate of Mountbatten, met him in a fishing hut along the Trika River. Hari Singh did not submit to persuasion by the viceroy that he must accede to either Pakistan or India. In the case of acceding to India, the viceroy promised to send the army to defend his borders. Mountbatten knew that Singh, being a practising Hindu, would not opt for Pakistan. The thrust was for him to join India, backed by a promise to defend the borders. (The defence apparently was necessary because he would go against his majority Muslim subjects and Pakistan may try to help them). Hari Singh evaded the reply by faking a stomach upset. He did not have the faith of his convictions and the mettle to press home his decision to be independent. This option the viceroy had refuted. In September, 1947, Lord Ismay tried to influence the Maharaja to make a decision without success.

Mountbatten decided to help India pick up the small states and merge them. On July 25th, 1947, he withdrew the protection given to Indian Princes in 1908 by the British government and the King. They were thrown into the mouths of nationalistic wolves. Kashmir, like all other states, was left to fend for herself. Mr Ram Chand Kak, prime minister of Kashmir, called for a standstill agreement and openly favoured Independent Kashmir or an Accession to Pakistan. He was removed from his post on August 11th, 1947, and was replaced by an army man, Janak Singh. Kak tried to escape but was apprehended and jailed in Srinagar. Foundations were already laid for Ram Chand Kak's fate by the memo Mountbatten carried with him to Kashmir. The brief to Mountbatten from Nehru was to remove Kak, release Abdullah from jail and for Kashmir to join the constituent assembly of India and not Pakistan.

Hari Singh in the meantime was distancing himself from the people. He unleashed heavy penalties in Poonch. In June 1947,

Sardar Mohammed Ibrahim Khan made the first militant organisation for armed insurrection against the Maharaja. He set the scene for the Sudhan revolt which caused the Pathan incursion.

On August 14th, 1947, the British paramountcy in Jammu and Kashmir came to a final end, and Kashmir was a free country. An agreement was signed by the Kashmiri government with Pakistan to run communications, the post and telegraph into Kashmir. The Pakistani flag was fluttering over the Srinagar post office. Janak Singh, the acting prime minister, ordered the flag to be brought down. Pakistan dispatched two emissaries, Dr Tasir and Sadiq Hassan to get the National Conference Party of Kashmir to support accession to Pakistan. They were not successful, in spite of being themselves Kashmiris and well received. Earlier, G.M. Sadiq led a delegation to visit Pakistan representing the National Conference. He was rebuffed and no one knows what part he played to vitiate relations with the leaders in Pakistan. Abdullah had been released from prison on September 20th, 1947 and was invited by both Mr Nehru and Mr Jinnah to visit and confer with them. He chose to go to India. Mr Nehru, as prime minister of India, received him at the airport *with a guard of honour*. He stayed with Nehru at his residence. There is a lot to read between the lines as events in the history of Kashmir have shown!

In August, 1947, Kashmir was visited by Indian leaders. Maharajas of Patiala, Kupurthala, and Faridkot came into Kashmir. Forces of Patalia regiment were dispatched into Kashmir as a result, in order to help Hari Singh. Mr Acharya Kriplani, the congressman and, significantly, Mahatma Gandhi himself, visited Kashmir. During this time other important changes were made. R C Kak, the prime minister, was sacked and replaced by Janak Singh first and soon after by pro-Indian Mehr Chand Mahajan. The British police chief was dismissed. Mahatma Gandhi asked the Maharaja to build a boat bridge over the River Ravi near Pathankote, and asphalt the road between Jammu and Kathua, so that troops and supplies could be rushed into Kashmir from India if need be. This road is independent of the two existing main arteries of communication which lead into Pakistan. India helped in upgrading the road linking Bagh in Poonch with the main Jhelum Valley Road near Chikar. This would enable traffic from India to enter through Noushahra to Kotli and remain open all year. Gurdaspur was already with India as allocated by Radcliffe's award. India could now have a straight run into Kashmir.

In September, 1947, the Sudhans of Poonch Kashmir, the great fighters in World War Two, rebelled against the ruler Hari Singh for his injustices. His minions were on a despoiling mission, burning and looting thousands of homes. The extortionate taxation rendered the people destitute. They grouped under the leadership of Sardar Abdul Quyum, a local landowner, and defeated the state army, taking full control of the local administration. In sheer desperation, the Maharaja's army torched the entire Poonch sector. The flames were visible from Murree, hundreds of miles away. The frustrated army returned from Poonch and persecuted half a million Muslims in Jammu, who were taken completely by surprise. There was a mass exodus of the Muslims into Pakistan. Many thousands of people, including women and children, were slaughtered in a pogrom hatched by Hari Singh and his ascendant priest, when they were assembled in one place and promised help to migrate, only to be killed.

The Maharaja, unable to bring himself to accede to either dominion and hoping the state would remain a 'Switzerland of Asia' signed a standstill agreement with Pakistan. During the latter part of September, 1947, Lord Ismay visited Kashmir and came to know of the covert agreement arrived at between Hari Singh, Mountbatten and Mr Nehru.

The Indian army was now bedding in through a backdoor approach. The Patalia regiment, a phalanx of the Indian army, entrenched itself in various parts of Jammu and Kashmir on October 17th, 1947 in preparation for an expected major conflict.

The Sudhan revolt, Jammu pogroms and consequent Pathan incursion had now started. On October 22nd, Kashmir was in complete darkness. Wazirstan elders declared jehad (holy war) and sent tribes voluntarily into Kashmir with 303 rifles. The Pathans were led by Sairab Khyat Khan, a twenty-four year old soldier. They defeated the state army and crossed the bridge to capture the powerhouse at Mohara Uri. The powerhouse was destroyed. A celebration party at the Maharaja's palace was interrupted with the blackout. *The party was over for the demagogue!* It heralded the beginning of the end for him and a century of autocratic Dogra rule.

British officers were still in command of both the Indian and Pakistani armies with a line of command linked to Auchinleck and Mountbatten sitting in Delhi. On October 24th, General Gracey Pakistan's Army Chief, informed General Lockhart, the Indian Army Chief by telephone that the Pathans had made an advance into Kashmir. Lockhart informed Mountbatten who in turn let Mr Nehru know about the situation. In the meantime Khyat Khan the twenty-four year old leader of the Pathans had crossed the vital bridge without a fight because the Muslims in Kashmir's state army had captured their officers and joined the tribals. General Gracey left the service at this crucial time and was replaced by Sir Frank Messervy. Parts of Kashmir liberated by Khyat Khan declared independence from the Maharaja's rule, and called themselves 'Azad Kashmir'. They formed an army, which, still in its teething state, advanced into Kashmir to join the Pathans.

The Maharaja packed his bags and left Kashmir overnight. He knew he had lost his throne and was defeated. His resolve against Indian pressure was tenuous. He was now amenable to accepting help. The Indian emissary, Mr Mennon, came with the offer. He was in Jammu by now and on Saturday, October 25th, at midnight, the Maharaja summoned his ADC: "Wake me up only if V.P. Mennon returns from Delhi, because that will mean India has come to my rescue. If he does not come before dawn, shoot me in my sleep with my service revolver." Mennon, sure enough, was there, because the revolver was not used! There is doubt as to whether he arrived after the Indian army had already flown into Srinagar.

There was tumultuous activity in Delhi and Mountbatten called an urgent meeting of the Defence Committee of India on October 25th and chaired it himself. General Rob Lockhart, Chief of Army staff, Admiral Hall and Air Marshal Elmhirst decided to invade Kashmir. General Bucher, GOC of Delhi, also known as 'viper under Nehru's pillow', had already prepared plans for the invasion and with General Russel, GOC of Punjab, carried them out in advance. The Indian army was already inside Kashmir.

It was therefore a mere formality to obtain a consent from the ruler of Kashmir. On Sunday October 26th, 1947, Mr V.P. Mennon was dispatched by Lord Mountbatten to obtain the signature on the document of accession to India from Maharaja Hari Singh. The document was supposed to state that the accession was subject to a formal plebiscite to be held when normal conditions were restored. Lord Mountbatten acted against the advice of the Supreme Commander, General Auchinleck, who was not in favour of the invasion. The Auk, as he was called, also wanted to airlift British citizens from Kashmir.

The war had begun and the Indian army was advancing fast into Pakistan's borders. Mr Jinnah ordered his Commander-in-Chief, Sir Douglas Gracey acting for General Messervey, to send troops into Kashmir to counteract the Indian incursion. The supreme commander of the joint Indo-Pakistani army was approached by Gracey and he advised against the Pakistani involvement. There were British officers on both sides! The British must have known about the imminent war. I suffered because I had to change from Cambridge education to the local system. The children in my class were British and they vanished one week before the war started. Our school in Srinagar was dissolved overnight.

Mr Jawaharlal Nehru, the Indian prime minister, was the force behind the decisions taken. Mr Mennon obtained the signature of the Maharaja claiming the credit for doing so. He declared: "Here it is. The bastard signed the act of accession. Now we have Kashmir, we will never let it go." He waved the document in one hand and a glass of whisky in the other. The assistant British High Commissioner, Alexander Symon, joined the toast.

Lord Mountbatten himself supervised the airlift of the army into Srinagar at the New Delhi airport on the October 27th. The Srinagar airport was ominously empty and inviting. The Punjab regiment was quickly deployed and a full scale combat ensued along the Baramulla road and suburbs. The Tribesmen were pushed out to the Uri hills. The Indian army was fast advancing both in Poonch and into the Baramula sectors.

General Gracey, the CIC of the Pakistan army, ignored orders to send troops into Kashmir. Gracey had been threatened by Mountbatten that he would lose his chance of a knighthood if he sent an army into Kashmir, as revealed by his personal assistant, Wilson. Sir Francis Mudie, Governor of Punjab, called Gracey a "wind-up merchant" for not honourably carrying out the orders of his boss, Mr

Jinnah. Gracey ordered that all British officers in the army would be withdrawn (Stand Down Order No 2) before a confrontation with the Indian army was possible... The supreme command in Delhi, Field Marshal Sir Claude Auchinleck (Auk) still controlled commanders in both countries and all parts of the army owed allegiance to the King up to June, 1948. Auk said he did not want British officers fighting against each other.

Mehr Chand Mahajan was a judge who worked for Radcliffe and was active in Kashmiri politics. He was supported by Sardar Patel in his appointment as the prime minister of Kashmir. Sheikh Abdullahwas made the Director General of administration. Mahajan soon gave way to Mr Abdullah to make a government. In the meantime, Hari Singh and his wife Tara Devi armed RSS activists and masterminded the 'Jammu Holocaust'. Muslims were trying to run away from armed RSS; many thousands were killed and their homes were wrecked. Mahajan, under instructions from Hari Singh, offered the fleeing Muslims safe passage to Pakistan. Half a million gathered in a place called 'Saubha'. A frightful pogrom left the place in eerie silence.

On *November 1st, 1947*, at a Lahore meeting between Mountbatten and Jinnah, the two governor generals met to discuss the Kashmir situation. The 'Three Point Solution' to the dispute proposed by Mr Jinnah was rejected by Mountbatten:

(i)   Azad Kashmir forces would be warned to stop fighting, otherwise both dominions would make war on them.

(ii) All armed forces would withdraw from Kashmir.

(iii) Both governor generals were to restore peace and hold a plebiscite.

Mountbatten said he had no authority to accept the proposals. The war was raging on.

Mr Nehru visited Kashmir on *November 2nd, 1947*. He addressed a mammoth public meeting in the red square. "We have declared that the fate of Kashmir is ultimately to be decided by the people. That pledge we have given and the Maharaja has supported it; it is not only a pledge to the people of Kashmir but to the world. We will not and cannot back out of it." The message was broadcast and the prime minister of Great Britain received a telegram endorsing the same pledge. He made no reference to the Lahore meeting with Mr Jinnah.

On *January 17th, 1948*, India approached the United Nations to seek a political solution to the armed conflict in Kashmir. She obtained the security council resolution for a ceasefire. India was now in de facto control of 54,000 square miles of Kashmir and the Pakistan part comprised 32,000 square miles. The Indian delegation to the UN was represented by Gopalaswami Ayyanger, Sheikh Abdullah M.C. Setalrad. A statement was made regarding the future of Kashmir: "Whether she should withdraw from India or accede to Pakistan or remain independent and claim membership of the United Nations is a matter for the unfettered decision by the people of the state after normal life is restored to them."

Kashmir was a subject of animated debate between the nations of the world. Proposals were put forward by various nations for a solution. On *January 24th, 1948*, Mr Warren Austen, from the United States of America, called for the establishment of an interim government in Kashmir to be followed by a plebiscite. The French proposals suggested a three point plan.

(i)   Withdrawal of foraying troops.

(ii) Return of inhabitants from around the world.

(iii) Establishment of administration which will guarantee free voting.

Mr Noel Baker of the United Kingdom stated, "These troubles came out of the history, I hope they will soon disappear into history again." Sir Percival Spear, elaborating further, made a reference to The 'Sale of Kashmir' to Gulab Singh in 1846, "The effects of this ill-omened act have not yet ceased to operate."

General McNaughton of Canada stated in the UN that, "The people of Kashmir should be permitted to express without fear or favour their wishes as to the future government of the state."

The pressure was mounting on India to relinquish control in Kashmir. Mr Nehru, in contemplating a resignation from his position as prime minister of India, writes to Mountbatten on *February 13th, 1948*, "I might consider my position in government. I have given pledges to the people of Kashmir and I do not propose to go against them." (Gopal Sarvepalli, *Jawaharlal Nehru, A Biography,* London, Jonathan Cape Ltd, 1979). Mr Nehru relied on support from his trusted friend, Sheikh Abdullah. Mr Abdullah was consolidating Indian positions in Kashmir and formed a government on *March 5th, 1948.* His cabinet took an oath of allegiance. Bakshi Gulam Mohammed, Mirza Afzal Beg, Gulam Mohammed Sadiq, Sardar Budh Singh, Shyam Lai Saraf, Girdari Lai Dogra and Pir Mohammed Khan were among the ministers.

The United Nations had a difficult task to find solutions acceptable to both sides. The sticking point was removing the military from the heads of Kashmiris. (It is the same today, almost fifty years on.) They passed resolution 9 (i) on *April 21st, 1948.*

The then USSR and the Ukraine abstained and Mr Nehru rejected it outright as unreasonable. The recommendations of the five member commission consisted of three major points:

(i)   That Pakistan secure a withdrawal of Pathans from Kashmir.

(ii)   Progressive withdrawal of the army by India. A small force to remain for law and order

(iii)   A coalition cabinet to be formed by the major parties and a Plebiscite administrator to be appointed to hold a free plebiscite.

NB: *chapter seven (Threat Of War) of the UN charter was not invoked.* Decisions could have been enforced. The UN were approached with an application to deal with the dispute under chapter six, which was mild and dealt with negotiations only.

July 27th, 1948: Winston Churchill wrote in a memo to Lord Atlee: "Britain's past pledges to the princes entitled Kashmir and Hydrabad to choose their own future by a plebiscite on the basis of adult suffrage under the auspices of the United Nations." (R.J. Moore, *Escape From Empire*, NY, Oxford University Press, 1983).

In the meantime, in order to consolidate its hold, India had to covertly plant trusted confederates in the state government. Mr Durga Prashad Dhar was one of them. He was made the home minister. One of the jobs he embarked on was to link Ladakh with India. He instructed Mr S. Narbo, the first qualified engineer from Ladakh, to expeditiously construct the Leh airstrip. This was a formidable task. Narbo complied and with the help of the Indian army he built the airstrip which proved so vital to India. The only viable link so far was through Srinagar. An alternative road to Ladakh via Himachal Pradesh is very precarious even with today's technology, but has been developed and used.

The UN was still struggling to solve the dispute. Field Admiral Chester W. Nimitz was appointed by the secretary general as plebiscite administrator, in March, 1949. The sticking point was the demilitarisation. President Truman of the USA and prime minister Atlee of Great Britain suggested Nimitz be the arbitrator. Pakistan accepted, but India refused, saying that no foreign arbitrators must intervene and, according to Mr Nehru, "Pakistani perfidy and her part in despoiling Kashmir are sought to be forgotten," and Pakistan must be taken as the invader. That was a condition for talks. Arbitration failed.

The United Nations' commission for India and Pakistan (UNCIP) did, however, manage to install a group of military observers in the area to maintain an armistice and investigate any violations along the five hundred mile long ceasefire line.

One more attempt at a reconciliation was made by General A.G.L. McNaughton of Canada, in December, 1949. He proposed to "retain Azad forces in Gilgat Baltistan" as a demilitarisation package. It was rejected by India. McNaughton, as president of the UN, tried to negotiate on a personnel level. Recriminations were repeated, reminiscent of the original diatribe.

It may be worth quoting some eminent Indian authors: "Nehru, the architect of foreign policy in India also used the occasion to back out of the commitment to hold the plebiscite in Kashmir." (Dilip Hero, 1949, *Inside India* Routledge 1976). Nehru maintained that Pakistan was the invader, "Pakistan's perfidy and her part in despoiling Kashmir are sought to be forgotten."

Sir William Barton stated in an article of the American *Foreign Affairs Quarterly,* that "...from the view point of population and geography, Kashmir is a part of Pakistan. Abdullah was Nehru's protégé. India would need an army of occupation to hold Kashmir.

India was economically weak and politically unstable and in a morass out of which lasting peace with Pakistan was the only escape." (Sisir Gupta, *Kashmir, A Study of Indo-Pakistan Relations*, January 1950).

The United Nations' efforts continued, despite setbacks. Australian Jurist, Sir Owen Dixon, was appointed as an UNCIP representative on *September 15th, 1950*. He worked hard against all odds to evolve an acceptable solution. Finally he came up with what became known as the 'Dixon Plan'. Jammu and Kashmir would be divided into four regions. Jammu and Ladakh would accede to India; Gilgat and Baltistan would remain with Pakistan. The Vale of Kashmir including Muzafarabad would have a plebiscite. New borders would be drawn up by an Indo-Pakistani boundary commission. The plan was rejected yet again.

January, 1951. Australian prime minister, Mr Robert Gordon Menzies, proposed a three-alternative plan to solve the military situation.

(i)   Station Commonwealth troops in Kashmir, or

(ii)   An Indo-Pakistani joint force, or

(iii)   Raise local troops in Kashmir.

India rejected the plan. Dr Frank Graham of the USA replaced Sir Dixon as an emissary of the United Nations in late 1951. His proposals were based on a simultaneous demilitarisation by India and Pakistan. As expected, they met the same fate and had an antithetical response from India.

The constant demurring attitude by India caused a proactive impasse. Mr Liaqat Ali Khan, the Pakistani prime minister, openly proposed that the "security council *impose* a solution on Kashmir". India rejected the proposal.

The UN support for a solution to the crisis was construed by India as western bias against India. In March, 1951, the Indian ambassador in Moscow, Mr Radha Krishenan, was explaining to them how the western countries were making a base against them in Kashmir. The USA and the UK under the pretext of rendering assistance through the UN had a vested interest. The purpose of these plans was the introduction of Anglo-American troops into the territory of Kashmir and to convert Kashmir into a colony. The stalling tactics from India were paying dividends for them. It left the last ditch attempts by mediators of the UN frustrated. India maintained that no arbitration would be accepted. The fate of the Kashmiri people would not be decided by a third party, the League of Nations, or an international Court of Justice at the Hague. India's own constitutional Article 51 does state that all disputes must be decided by arbitration. (Not for Kashmir!)

While the world was debating the fate of Kashmir, Abdullah's government was ruling in comfort. In *September to October, 1951*, the constituent assembly elections were called in the state of Jammu and Kashmir for everyone over twenty-one. The seventy-five deputies would be returned, forty-five from Kashmir and Ladakh, and thirty from Jammu. Elections were very simple. In Kashmir, forty-three seats were elected unopposed, two independents withdrew under pressure, there was no need for balloting. In Jammu, thirteen nomination papers of Praja Prashad, the opposition party, were rejected because of a fallacy in filling them out. On October 12th Praja Prashad boycotted the election, accusing the government of illegal practices.

Mr Nehru was irate at the British and snapped at them, saying, "I fear I am a little tired of their good intentions and good offices!" This was in response to a statement from the British government made on *April 7th, 1952*, that the official stand remained "... reduction of the Indian military in Kashmir."

July 24th, 1952. Nehru-Abdullah Agreement. The prime ministers of Kashmir and India conferred in Delhi and signed an agreement:

(i) The state assembly will elect a head of state for a term of five years. (Not a governor nominated by the President of India, as is normal for other states).

(ii) The state will look after its own security and execute its own land reforms.

(iii) The state will have powers to define and regulate the rights and privileges of permanent residents of the state.

(iv) Indians will not acquire land in the state.

(v) The state flag can be kept. The Indian flag will be supreme.

(vi) The President of India will invoke Article 352 of the Indian
Constitution only if the state government will request it.
Accordingly, in the case of invasion, or violent uprising, a
state of emergency will only be declared at the request of the
state government.

Mr Nehru had built his Kashmir policy around Abdullah. It was
his commitment to India and secularism which justified prompt
military action.

'Abdullah saw possibilities of an Independent Kashmir, with
guarantees from both the USA and the UK after meeting Mrs Loy
Henderson, the wife of the American ambassador in Delhi and some
CIA agents.' This was a rumour spread by some Indian politicians.
Mr Abdullah has denied these allegations.

The UN saga was still simmering when Mr Nehru, deliberating
with Graham at Geneva on *August 7th, 1952*, said, "Kashmir is so
important strategically that India and Pakistan, as well as other
powers, will continue to be interested and this struggle for influence
will ensure that Kashmir is neither independent nor peaceful nor
normal." Alive today, Mr Nehru would have said on Kashmir, 'See!
I told you so.'

Mr Abdullah, in the meantime, was having his roots splayed by a
melange of political factions working against him. The Praja Prashad
(Jana Sang) party in Jammu launched an anti-Abdullah campaign in
late 1952. The agitators were arrested. The Indian minister, Mr
Ayyanger, intervened on behalf of and in favour of the Hindu agitators
of Jammu, but no word was said for the thousands of Muslims also
held in jails for demonstrating.

Mr Abdullah felt a jolt in his heart and his misgivings against New
Delhi were getting stronger. It was now becoming clear to him that
the semi-autonomy of Kashmir was being eroded. Mr Jawaharlal
Nehru visited Kashmir on *May 16th, 1953*. "To my utter amazement,
he [Nehru] suggested summoning the constituent assembly to ratify the
accession to India," writes Sheikh Abdullah (*Flames Of Chinar*). "I
reminded him of our public and formal commitment regarding a

plebiscite. I was amazed to see him speaking quietly with Bakshi Gulam Mohammed and his friends, whispering surreptitiously."

It was soon after this visit, on *June 23rd, 1953*, that Mr Shyama Prashad Mukerji, the Hindu Mahasaba leader, defied the formality of obtaining a permit to enter Kashmir from India. He was arrested, and died in prison due to natural causes. There was an outcry in India and more support was expressed for a full merger of Kashmir with India. Trouble was brewing for the Sheikh. On *August 9th, 1953*, Sheikh Mohammed Abdullah the incumbent prime minister of Kashmir, was arrested while in office. Col. B.M. Kaul came from the Indian army to oversee the arrest. The Sheikh was replaced by his own second-in-command, Bakhshi Gulam Mohammed. He was accused of treason and revolt against the authorities in India, an irony of fate exemplified. I was reminded of the guard of honour Abdullah received in India not many years back! It may have been the same soldiers who arrested him!

Abdullah was not expecting the deliberate and systematic erosion of autonomous status and felt deceived by his confederate friends in Delhi. Mr Bakhshi received very big sums of money from India to lavish on the people and feather his own nest and those of his family. Abdullah, 'Lion Of Kashmir', who 'thought' like a socialist but acted like a 'dictator', was manoeuvred as a petty Machiavellian and succumbed at the hands of his long associate-in-arms. He was released for three months on *January 8th, 1958*, and re-arrested. A bogus case was lodged against him and his associates for conspiracy to import arms and start an insurrection in collusion with Pakistan. It only served to reveal Indian deceptions towards Kashmir. "Abdullah on trial but India in the dock," reported *The Observer* from London on December 16th, 1963. The case was dropped.

Unfortunately, putting the lion in the cage did not take away the Kashmir problem. Mr Nehru now, for the first time, agreed to talk to Pakistan. The Pakistani prime minister, Mohammed Ali and Mr Nehru meet in Delhi on *August 20th, 1953*. The Delhi Agreement was signed. In a joint communiqué it was agreed that a plebiscite would be held and a plebiscite administrator would be appointed by the end of *April, 1954*. Demilitarisation would start with the advice of their military experts. No action was taken by either country.

India, by now, had come to a stage of claiming Kashmir to be an integral part of that country. The United Nations, in sheer frustration, unanimously agreed on a proposal in *November, 1953*, that once and for all it would get an opinion from the General Assembly or the international Court of Justice about the legal validity of Kashmir's accession to India. Solutions were predicated to the presence of goodwill. India refused. It became clear that Kashmir was on the road to a radical left-wing totalitarian dictatorship. Mr Abdullah would spearhead the doctrine. His opponents called him a 'communalist' in Kashmir – 'Communist' in Jammu – and a 'nationalist' in India!

August 9th, 1955: Mirza Afzal Beg, Mr Abdullah's lieutenant, set up a new party called the Plebiscite Front. The main demand of the party was a plebiscite in Kashmir. The party was banned by India but carried the day with popular support.

India was trying to find every possible avenue of support for their policy on Kashmir. The government invited the Russians to visit Kashmir. In *December, 1955*, the head of the Communist party, Nikita Khrushchev and prime minister of the USSR, Bulganin, visited Kashmir. They reiterated their position on Kashmir and said that Kashmir was an integral part of India. Khrushchev said, "We are so near that if ever you call us from your mountain tops we will appear at your side." They were given a great reception in Kashmir. The Russians killed two birds with one stone. They defied the western powers to have a possible base in Kashmir and they brought India along in their fold – a great potential for Communism with nearly a billion starving people potentially red in tooth and claw!

The Kashmiri assembly of the puppet government was under pressure to pass a resolution and ratify the instrument of accession to India. That was obediently carried out. The Security Council rejected the resolution passed by the Jammu and Kashmir constituent's assembly on *January 24th, 1957*. The resolution passed by the Kashmir assembly stated that Jammu and Kashmir, as an integral part of India, was a violation of the principal of a plebiscite.

Mr Gunner Jarring was sent into the subcontinent to renew attempts to negotiate a settlement. Mr Feroz Khan Noon, of Pakistan, agreed to withdraw the army from all parts of Kashmir if they were replaced by UN forces. The resolution was rejected by India but backed by the USSR.

The misgivings and disputations between the public and the incumbent government revived and it became obvious to people that the terms of reference and promises made by India were actually spurious, and Kashmir along with her people was being taken for a ride. The general attitude of the Indian officers working in Kashmir and the alienation between the two communities was simmering into a volcano.

The following sequence of events put fuel into the fire already ignited:

1. On *January 8th, 1958*, Sheikh Mohammed Abdullah was released from prison without any prior indication and made a significant statement: "Mr Nehru had no business speaking on behalf of Kashmir. Kashmir's accession to India had lost its validity after my dismissal. Bakhshi could shout from the top of the Banihal Pass that Kashmir's accession to India was final, but his government comprises Goondas [vandals] and thieves. Most members of the Kashmir constituent assembly were forced to accept the constitution of India. It was only the people who could decide." He was promptly arrested again until April, 1964.

2. *1958*: Indian Administrative and Police services, IAS and IPS, were incorporated into Kashmir. This was a shock to young officers aspiring to climb the ladder to high positions. Two centuries of Sikh and Dogra rule had sealed the fate of the Muslim youngsters, because they were not permitted an education or a government job at the end. This was another nail in the coffin of their relations with the Indian rule.

3. It was about this time that the authority of the Auditor General of India was imposed on the state. The feeling was that India had reneged on its promise of letting people in Kashmir have full control of their finances and economy.

4. *1959*: The census control of the Indian government was imposed on Kashmir.

5. *1960*: The judiciary in Kashmir was accountable to a local legal system, always independent of any other country. The Supreme Court of India jurisdiction was extended into Kashmir.

6. *1961*: The industries which mattered for Kashmir were forest, horticulture, and agriculture based. The control of licensing an industry from these sources now came from India. Natural resources and raw materials were carted across into India. No industry except for a small watch-making factory was permitted or allowed to survive.

7. *August, 1962*: China invaded Kashmir and penetrated deep inside Ladakh, pushing the Indian army stationed there into retreat. On September 8 of this year, the Chinese in a blatant manner crossed the McMoahan Line passing through the Thag La Ridge. On October 20th, having tested the Indian response and their strength, the Chinese invaded Kashmir, Nefa, Ladakh and Barahoti. They made a swift advance along the Indus and Shyok rivers, snapping up Chip Chap Valley, Lake Pangog and Demchok. There was little resistance offered. They maintain their occupation of a part of Kashmir, Aksai Chin, even today as I write. Kashmir will always have its claim on Aksia Chin. It is important for its ancestral ties with its people, its shawl industry and traditional trade.

8. *December, 1962 to May, 1963*: Six sessions of negotiations took place between India and Pakistan over Kashmir. They were all futile.

9. *1963*: The China-Pak agreement on boundaries in Azad Kashmir concluded. Territory ceded to China was subjected to final settlement of the future of Kashmir.

10. *August, 1963*: Mr Nehru made a statement that "Concessions offered to Pakistan are no longer open and must be treated as withdrawn." The next time India and Pakistan met was on a battlefield. Indian leaders were getting worried about the implications of a perpetual stand-off with the UN and Pakistan. The prominent politician, Rajagopal Achari, made a statement on Kashmir. "The accession of Kashmir took

place under conditions of great peril. It was not the intention to claim it as an irrevocable affiliation." (1964)

11. *1964*: The Indian government decided it was about time that laws were made for presidents' rule to extend into Kashmir. The need for this legislation was presumably felt because the ripple effect of the turbulence begun in Kashmir was reaching political circles in Delhi. The incumbent puppet governments in Kashmir could now be dissolved and replaced from Delhi at the flick of a finger. It is for that purpose that articles 356 and 357 came into force in Kashmir.

12. *1965*: The Indian labour law became enforceable. The only industry employing labour was in Jammu and fortunately the law did not require its enforcement.

13. The excessive Indian armed police and military in Kashmir were hostile by their mere presence in the streets of the inner cities. 'Wherever you go in the valley, no Kashmiri armed forces are in evidence,' (P.N. Bazaz, *The Crucible*, Delhi, Kashmir Publishing House, 1964.)

14. *1966*: A representative was chosen from Kashmir for the lower house of parliament in Delhi. The promise of a devolved state of Jammu and Kashmir was now completely eroded.

15. *1969*: The dreaded Unlawful Activities Act, Article 248 was enforced. The people could now feel the effects of repression and some of those who had lived through the Dogra regime were now comparing notes. The more powerful TADA came into force later to replace the infamous 248.

These are the important landmarks in the recent history of Kashmir which leave poignant memories for its people. They feel beguiled and shattered, because this time it was their own people who promised a secure and sound life to them. Now they have to go back a hundred years and start again!

December 1963: The sacred relic was stolen from the Hazratbal Shrine. Millions of people came out in the streets of Kashmir and demonstrated their solidarity to protest against the sacrilege.

The relic was recovered and identified by religious ascendants. This incident left a lasting impression on people who observed what the tides do to Kashmiri politics. Kashmiris will not accept any decision imposed on them as peremptory. They are a force to reckon with.

China has always supported Kashmir in her self-determination. Chou En-lai made a statement that people in Kashmir have been treated perfidiously. In February, 1964, Mr Chen Yi, the foreign minister of China, visited Pakistan and endorsed an open support for a plebiscite in Kashmir.

India was making every possible move to calm the situation down in Kashmir. Sheikh Abdullah was released from prison for no apparent reason on *April 8th, 1964*. On *May 17th, 1964*, he went to Pakistan with Pandit Nehru's blessing. His entourage comprised his confederates, Mubarak Shah from Baramula, Mubarak Shah Naqashbandi the famous judge, close associate Afzal Beg, Choudry Mohammed Shafi, Begsheri and his son, Farooq. In Pakistan he met Moulvi Yousuf Shah, Mirwise of Kashmir now in exile, after many years. He also met his old jail mate Choudry Gulam Abbas. He gave president Ayub Khan the classical string instrument 'santoor' as a present from Kashmir. The delegation made an impression on the president and he agreed to visit India and meet Mr Nehru. "India and Pakistan must come together as friends," the president told the delegation and pleaded for a negotiated settlement. Bad luck does not strike once for Kashmir: Mr Jawaharlal Nehru died while Sheikh Abdullah was still in Pakistan.

The Indian political scene changed. Kashmiri politics were pushed further into a maelstrom. No one in India had the charisma to take a decision on Kashmir, not least of which was giving her people the right of a plebiscite. Mr Abdullah intensified his campaign more openly against Indian occupation than during his friend Nehru's lifetime. In March, 1965, he and his associate, Mr Afzal Beg, met Mr Chou En-lai, prime minister of China, in Algeria. They went to Cairo and met President Gamal Nasser and pleaded for support from the Afro-Asian countries, in favour of self-determination for the people of Kashmir. They met King Faisal of Saudi Arabia, who openly supported self-determination for the people of Kashmir. They were offered a Pakistani passport to travel to Peking. Abdullah published a 'Foreign Affairs' article in which he mentioned "Nehru's repeated promises of a plebiscite in Kashmir." He made a statement about various possible solutions for Kashmir:

1. Overall plebiscite.

2. Independence of whole state.

3. Independence with joint control of foreign affairs by India and Pakistan.

4. Dixon's Plan and partition of the state and plebiscite in the Valley.

5. Independence of the Valley.

He did not mention union with India as an option. Sheikh Abdullah arrived back in India and the 'lion' was promptly put back in his cage. They were waiting for him at the airport. He spent the next three years in Kodai Kanal Jail.

Azad Kashmir forces were getting desperate for any sight of a solution and decided to enter Kashmir.

In *September, 1965*, armed volunteers penetrated Indian army files and fought open battles with them. The army burnt down to absolute ashes a whole locality. Batamalu in Srinagar was gutted in order to capture the militants. No one was caught. A deadly war broke out between India and Pakistan. Both sides claimed victory. The pressure was on for the UN to act now that the two countries had come to blows and lost thousands of men between them.

On *September 4th, 1965*, a UN resolution was passed and India and Pakistan were asked to stop the war, and resolve the underlying dispute of Kashmir. The fighting came to a stop, but the cause of the conflict still simmered on.

On *January 10th, 1966*, The Tashkant Declaration was signed by India and Pakistan. Both countries agreed to affirm not to wage war against each other, to go back to the 1965 line of control, not to interfere in each other's internal affairs, not to wage propaganda against each other, to exchange diplomats, have economic and trade relations, exchange POWs, discuss refugees and meet at the highest level. Bad luck for Kashmir struck again. Mr Lal Bahadur Shatri, the prime minister of India, suddenly died and with him the fragile peace initiative. He negotiated peace with Pakistan at Tashkant but did not live to see it through.

The stalemate continued. India started getting tough and declared the Plebiscite Front party in Kashmir unlawful. Many of its remaining leaders were arrested. The party was demanding a plebiscite in Jammu, Kashmir and Ladakh, and Sheikh Abdullah was the force behind it.

On *January 30th, 1971*, the Indian Airline plane flying from Srinagar to Delhi was hijacked. This sparked off yet another armed conflict between India and Pakistan, this time in East Pakistan. India accused Pakistan of helping the hijackers. The fourteen-day war culminated in the creation of Bangladesh.

Indira Gandhi was the prime minister of India. She was very reticent to any compromises for Kashmiris. She had grown up with Kashmir being administered by India. She spent all her holidays in Kashmir and had spring water from Chashma Shahi flown in everyday for her personnel use. What transpired between her father and the rest of the world was of only historical interest to her. She was responsible for the creation of Bangladesh. It was after the war that she agreed to meet Pakistani leaders for a ceasefire.

The Simla Agreement was signed between India and Pakistan on July 3rd, 1972. The important points of the agreement were:

(i)   Restore normal relations.

(ii) POWs of Pakistan to be returned. Pakistani army had conceded defeat.

(iii) Talk about disputes and arrive at amicable solutions.

(iv) Both sides to respect the line of control in Kashmir.

Mrs Indira Gandhi was known to have an invincible fervour for power. This got a boost after the Bangladesh war. The Russians were spurring her on. She gave orders to test a nuclear bomb. In *May, 1974*, India exploded a nuclear device. The cost of this project was in the region of $1.5 billion!

Mrs Gandhi showed her mettle by having the Lion tamed. Abdullah, who was like an old uncle to her, was forced to accept the position of Chief Minister of Kashmir. He had been deposed as prime minister, but she did not like two prime ministers in one country, which had important political implications for Kashmir. Mrs Gandhi went further and made the Sheikh reinforce the seal of accession.

In *February, 1975*, the 'Kashmir Accord' was agreed to and the great myth underlying article 370 was exposed. It was made known that article 370 can in fact be abrogated and changed by the president of India by virtue of article 254 of the Indian constitution, *any time*. Moulvi Farooq, a young Muslim leader in Kashmir, (made Mirwise by Bakhshi at the age of fourteen) opposed the accord. Moulvi was later lured by the Congress and Janata Dal party to join hands against Abdullah and his government.

In the midst of this chaos, and mounting pressures, Sheikh Mohammed Abdullah, the invincible lion of Kashmir became ill with heart disease and he died while in office from natural causes. The funeral was attended by a large crowd of people and among others, Mrs Indira Gandhi, the prime minister of India, accompanied the procession. The coffin was draped with the Indian flag. It was not long after his death in 1982, that his son Farooq celebrated his coronation and took charge of the government.

Dissent was simmering in the grass roots of Kashmir. Abdullah's departure made it possible for repressed feelings to surface. The young political activists were getting ebullient and ready to take up arms. A resistance movement was burgeoning. The more prominent activists were apprehended. Young men like Shabir Ahmad Shah, Azam Inqalabi, Ahsan Dar, Yasin Mallik, Javed Mir, Shakil Bakhshi, Mushtaq Zargar and others, were liaising with comrades like Amanuila Khan, Farooq Rahmani, Gulam Qadir and others, from across the border and were all getting known. Some of the most remarkable young heroes of Kashmir willingly gave their lives for the good of their country. There are an estimated 45,000 people either buried in martyrs' graveyards or missing altogether, since the uprising started in 1989, but names like Maqbool Bhat, Ashfaq Majid, Hamid Sheikh, Doctors Abdul Ahad Guru, and Farooq Ashai, Prof. Abdul Ahad, Nasir Bukhtiyar, Arif Shuja Mallik, A.R. Ishali, Dr Abrar or Aziz ur Rehman, to mention only a few, will always be remembered in the history of Kashmir. There are others whose lives are on the line and are facing torture in Indian jails. The numbers are unknown but a delegation of lawyers visiting some prisons reported ill treatment of some outstanding youths now incarcerated. Mushtaq Zargar, Sheikh Abdul Aziz, Mushtaq ul Islam, Lodhi Bilal, and Mohammed Yasin Bhat are a few of the well-known.

In *February, 1984*, Mr Mohammed Maqbool Bhat was hanged in Tihar Jail, Delhi. Mr Bhat was the founder member of the Jammu and Kashmir Liberation Front. The Front is seeking an independent Jammu and Kashmir. Maqbool Bhat was executed on 6th of February. The death penalty existed from an old prosecution.

In *January, 1990*, the last vestige of the government of Kashmir ended without any warning. Mr Jagmohan was installed as governor of Kashmir and took over its administration expeditiously. This was the beginning of the long drawn-out saga of crucibles for Kashmiris. Demonstrations and processions, people shouting slogans of freedom and holding banners demanding an end to the Indian rule were seen all over the Valley. The governor responded by ordering the army out and shooting at any assembly of people. This resulted in mass massacres well documented by human rights organisations.

Kashmir, Doda, Kishtiwar and the Poonch areas of the state are under siege and ruled by the gun. Pogroms, mass rapes and barbaric custodial killings are in evidence as the sinews of militarism and power. Kashmir has been described as the Killing Fields of Asia, the Human Abattoir for India, and a Heaven on Fire, by others. The limited scope of this book will not allow a full report on all the atrocities committed in Kashmir; it may be expedient however, to mention a few incidents to exemplify the magnitude of the travesty.

Mass raping of women, young and old, by the Indian army took place in Chanapora Srinagar Kashmir on *March 7th, 1990*. The matter was widely reported.

On *January 21st, 1990*, a demonstration of people in Basant Bagh and the Gauw Kadal area, shouting slogans, was stopped by the army and two hundred people were killed in one burst of gunfire. It was only the next day, January 22nd, when the funeral procession carrying the dead was joined by masses of grieving people, and as the funeral was approaching the Hawal district, the army surrounded them and opened indiscriminate fire, killing another forty people. The street was covered with a river of blood. The coffins were perforated with bullet holes.

Similar massacres with many hundreds of innocent people murdered in cold blood have been perpetrated in Tengpora, Khanyar, Islamia School, Srinagar, outside Medical Institute, in Bijbehara and Badgam. The recent massacre of one Muslim family in Doda Kashmir where five in the family were murdered in cold blood was admitted by the authorities.

Amnesty International, Asia Watch and International Alert were repeatedly denied permission to visit Kashmir in order to investigate reports of brutal military and police violations of Human Rights.

Kashmir Huriyat conference was formed with an affiliation of 32 various political parties and militant groups. Moulvi Omar Farooq, the twenty year old son of the late Moulvi Farooq, was chosen as its chairman. The phalanx of senior members of the Huriyat, Syed Ali Shah Geelani, Abdul Gani Lone, Professor Abdul Gani, G.M. Safi and others, have been reinforced by powerful leaders like Shabir Shah, Yasin Mallik, Javed Mir, Shakil Bakhshi. There are political activists like Hashim Qureshi living in exile controlling political parties affiliated to Huriyat. There are other veterans of Kashmir politics like Azam Inqalabi, Dr Gulam Qadir Wani, Farooq Rahmani, Inayat Ulla Andrabi, and leaders from the Azad Kashmir like Amanullah Khan, Sardar Abdul Qayyum who are playing a crucial role in the struggle for political freedom of Jammu and Kashmir.

The Indian government has been under pressure from the international community to evolve a process for the resolution of the Kashmir dispute. India has made a start. Shabir Shah, the prisoner of Conscience, Yasin Mallik, the JKLF president, Shakil Bakhshi and recently, Javed Mir have been released. A political process has been promised by India. The people of Kashmir and the rest of the world are waiting!

On 'Kashmir Day', the 5th of February, 1996, life in the whole country of Pakistan and both sides of Kashmir froze to a standstill. The solution for Kashmir is no nearer today than it was in 1947. Nuclear arms races, prithvi missiles and atomic tests by India and counter measures by Pakistan have made a peaceful solution remote.

In the meantime, seven more people were killed on this day in Kashmir and in this week an Indian rocket attack killed twenty-two people in Azad Kashmir. The Indian government have been ruling Kashmir through a military based administration and a governor appointed from Delhi for the last six years, which is a direct violation of the tenets of their own constitution. They have recently announced that they will hold elections in the state to install a government under the Indian constitution, a move considered to be a farce by many observers. These elections will presage more violence. *The crusade for the freedom of Kashmir goes on unabated.*

SUFFERING AND ABUSE

Buffeted Baby Syndrome

The people of Kashmir want a separate home! They have suffered abuse from despotism and felonies inflicted on them, from as far back as history goes.

Over the years, thousands of Kashmiris have perished or languished in jails for the crime of speaking out for a redress of their grievances. The constant sense of fear always keeps lurking in their minds. Invasions after invasions for thousands of years and the milieu of repression they have endured leave them with retroactive reflections of cataclysm and the impending fear. About AD 500, Khukhs, a tribal bunch of looters, descended upon Kashmir, and killed and plundered like savages. It is common for people even nowadays to reprimand children with threats of "Khuhks are knocking on the door!" and it works to frighten them. People may have woken up to the realities of the present world but the livid memories are still alive, passed down from the elders.

"My forefathers for many generations were subjected to wanton torture all through their lives. My parents lived through the humiliation of a servile existence. They had to play second fiddle to a phantom regime planted by big feudal masters sitting in Delhi. I have experienced in my young life the sinews of militarism in administration and the erosion of my self esteem. I will not allow my son to slog through the odyssey of servitude and inherit obeisance to foreign rule." These were the words of Farooq Papa, a militant leader, when I visited him at his hideout in Kashmir. "If it means my death, so be it," he said. These are the slogans which reverberate in the labyrinth of this society. A downward gaze, inquisitorial of the world, into the rampant abuse of these people, will splay the roots of morality and concern for fellow human beings.

Human Bondage

You live or drift a life forlorn

Body and mind, frayed and torn

Turning the leaves of years bygone

Wounds of torment, sinew and bone

Forays from south, the worst ever known

Marauding, plundering as history has shown

From north and west and east alike

With swords and spears out to strike

So endearing and caring, Why Kashmir?

So blissful, so delightful, a deluge of peace!

Human bondage, transcends greed!

Ignorant hectors cannot perceive.

Majid Siraj

The extent to which the people of Kashmir have been used as objects for torture and humiliation is described in chronicles filling the shelves of many archives. They were exploited in bonded servitude and suffered interminable abuses of their basic rights as human beings. Their inherent propensity for endurance was responsible for their survival. The abuse inflicted was both in physical as well as in mental forms. Hazlitt's book, *The Life of Napoleon Bonaparte*, back in the mid-nineteenth century, sums up conditions in Kashmir. "The peasants were overworked, half-starved, treated with hard words and hard blows, subjected to unceasing extractions and every species of petty tyranny."

Mihira Kula was called the 'White Hun', who behaved like the Asiatic people of the fourth century when they destroyed Europe. People received every form of the torment as if they were destined for it.

Kashmir can claim distinction in the number of invasions, the magnitude of the tyranny, the depth of anarchy and the cruel exploitation it has undergone during different periods of its history. In AD 939 the King of Kashmir, Unmattavati administered torture upon his subjects by extraordinary and brutal means.

1087: King Harisha imposed the most punitive forms of taxation. The poor were having to work harder still and then starve to death.

Zulfi Khan from Mongolia invaded Kashmir and set fire to every house he looted. The aftermath was as if ashes and cinders left were those after a catastrophic fire. Zulfi perished with 50,000 people he enslaved, crossing the Devasar Pass.

The agony for Kashmir went on as people picked up the pieces again until the next invasion came along.

1752: Ahmad Shah Abdali from Afghanistan marauded into Kashmir and caused havoc with the people. The victory of the invasion sent his head spinning with power. The natives were there to be used, and abused. Every morsel of food was snatched from their mouths in order to pay the ruler. Abdali was a tyrant and people dreaded the sound of his name.

Afghans having left, people clamoured for a respite and helped the Sikhs to rule.

1819: Ranjit Singh, the Sikh ruler from Punjab never visited Kashmir. He sent his Sikh governors to administer Kashmir. They unleashed a reign of terror.

One evening, in this savage rule, the Sikh governor was getting inebriated on alcohol, when the French traveller Jacquemont called on him. He blatantly bragged to his guest about his exploits with locals. "I hanged two hundred Kashmiris in my first year of office for no better reason than to frighten others off." He talked about the unique methods of torture he had used. There never was any let-up in the misery inflicted on the people. Joseph Wolf, a preacher, described how people were fleeing Kashmir tortured, and humiliated. "We are bought and sold like pieces of bread," they said. This went on during the time of Sher Singh, Ranjit's own son who was sent in as governor in 1832.

The Sikh rule ended in 1846 to the great relief of the people. The amnesty did not last for long. The British, having won Kashmir from Sikhs, sold it to Gulab Singh. People resisted Gulab Singh's rule, the first Dogra ruler, and fought him off, in the hope that a kinder rule from the inside would prevail. They wanted to live in peace. Gulab Singh sought the help of the mighty British forces and succeeded in enslaving with shackles the Kashmiri people for the next hundred years. Gulab Singh believed that he was a progeny from the Solar dynasty, the supreme ruling class, from the line of Brahma (creator). The offspring of Brahma, Manu, had nine sons, even though he was a bisexual. The eldest of the nine, was also androgynous and had two names, Ila and Ilaa, depending on which sex form was presented at the time. The Solar clan were the rulers and the lunar class were the ruled. Gulab was a Solar but, androgynous or not, he created havoc with the lives of innocent people in Kashmir!

The repressive measures he unleashed were intended to keep all local people subservient, poor, deprived and terrified. The taxations were heavy. No local Muslim was allowed in government service or the state army. The slaughter of cows was a capital offence. Gulab Singh went into the prison to witness for himself punishment inflicted on the prisoners. He had some victims flayed alive under his own eyes, the bodies cut open and stuffed with straw. He then ordered the bodies to be planted on the wayside so that passers-by could see them! Prisoners murdered in this way could be those Muslims who had slaughtered a cow or stolen food. This gruesome punishment was designed to instil terror and authority in his subjects. He called his son to witness this ordeal and take a lesson in the act of governing. Rambir Singh, his son, succeeded him with all this grooming and took over the "Torture Chambers". A lamentable legacy which the people will not forget.

People were incarcerated in their own country and had no choice but to endure all the hardships inflicted by the ruler. The slave labour, the hideous punishments, and the purgatory of forced destitution left no alternatives for them except to propitiate under duress and withdraw into faith in God. Sufferance for them was understood as "divine punishment" for a flaw in their faith or a sin they may have committed or their parents may have been responsible for! The people of Kashmir like no other community of the world are known for their invincible faith in God. They are *Zulum Parast*, or worshippers of tyranny, as described by some writers. Kashmiri author, Gwasha Nath Kaul, described the conditions in the capital of Kashmir: "There are two prostitution centres in Tashwan and Gao Kadal. Begging, cheap labour, disease, deaths, dirty clothes are a common feature. Pandits look 5% better off. 90% of the Muslim homes were mortgaged to Hindu money lenders (Sahukars)."

The saga of repression, torture and extortion continued for the next century under Dogra rule. In 1941, 93.4% of the people were illiterate, and until 1945 the per capita income was Rs 74.8 per annum, (£1.50). During this time the Maharaja's court spent Rs 4 million expenditure on his army, which was more than Rs 5 million per year. The Dogra regime systematically exploited the poor Muslims. Fruit, birch bark, tobacco, hides, saffron, violets, silk and water nuts were some of the items monopolised by the state from which the Brahmins deducted a heavy percentage before the rest went into the treasury. The Muslims were treated as serfs.

To be a 'Beggar' was a form of forced labour which the young men had to undertake, if the ruler wanted to build a road or a bridge. No wages were paid and anyone found guilty of non-compliance was beaten up with lathis (bamboo sticks) or taken into prison and tortured. Pundit Jawaharlal Nehru made a statement against the 'reign of terror' Maharaja Hari Singh had unleashed. "The wanton police firing, bodies doused with petrol and burnt, the wounded thrown into jails instead of hospitals. Srinagar is the *'City of the dead'*." People were made to *crawl on the streets* and shout slogans. As the cliché goes that 'history repeats itself', similar methods of humiliation were used by General Dyer in Punjab to crush any anti-British revolt. Half a century later this type of atrocity was repeated on the subjects of Kashmir, again in crackdown operations of the Indian army.

Politics was a luxury Kashmiris could not afford, but got mired with by chance. 1924 saw the first ever seeds of political awareness sown, with the workers' strike in a Srinagar silk weaving factory and the formation of the 'Reading Room' established by Sheikh

Mohammed Abdullah and his associates. Politics emerged as a feature in society. As can be imagined, the feeling amongst the masses was a sudden passion to campaign for freedom from slavery and the rebirth of a life with dignity. Unfortunately for the people of Kashmir, *politics heralded an era of more suffering*. They now had to face the army in the streets. Thousands were shot dead, point blank. Many thousands were tortured in prisons. The British had washed their hands of Kashmir. They, having conquered it from the Sikhs in the first place, had then sold it to Gulab Singh for a paltry sum. They decided to stay away from Kashmir. Kashmir was perceived in legendary tales as a place of 'snakes' with all its attending hazards of its non-ethical bordering countries. China, Russia, Afghanistan and Mongolia were perceived as potential predators. The idea was to let someone else do the fighting against invaders and from a distance the British would still maintain paramount power over the state. Kashmir would have otherwise been ruled directly by the British. That may have changed the total course of history for Kashmir. Kashmir would have been a part of British India and at the time of independence, demarcation lines would have been drawn through it by Percival Radcliffe, for its destiny with India or Pakistan. It was after a great struggle with the Dogra rulers that the British finally succeeded in installing a Resident in Kashmir during Partap Singh's rule. On *November 12th, 1931*, B.J. Glancy was appointed to set up a commission to inquire into the grievances of Kashmiri Muslims. Glancy had served in Kashmir and already knew the problems. This 'Glancy Commission' relieved the misery to a large extent. In its formation, other members from the community were incorporated. Mr Gulam Ahmad Ashai, Choudry Ghulam Abbas, Prem Nath Bazaz and Pandit Lok Nath Sharma were the nominated members. The educational rights for all and property rights to farmers were recommended by the commission. These laws affected Pandits who came out in revolt, especially against the land reform. Protests were organised and were lead by Jia Lal Kilam. The agitation was quashed. For the first time some local Muslims were brought into government service. Some of the repressive laws were repealed. The slaughtering of cows was punished with a life sentence instead of death by hanging, and forced labour laws were changed. The educational institutions and hospitals were started by the church missionaries.

Mental Abuse

Kashmir has always been a land of wandering divas, intellectual fakirs and saints detached from the world. In medical terms, the hospitals have been filled with reactive depressive disorders, psycho-neurosis and dementia. The constant fear of abuse and persistent insecurity lead to these problems. Large numbers of cannabis oasis-like little clubs were allowed to open and were full of users. The habit was rampant and made legal with the intention of keeping down all insurgency. In 1990, there was an upsurge in the incidence of major psychosis in the community. Daily war-like conditions and the total breakdown of law and order frightened little boys running for cover from the military firing at them. It was a case of fright by day and subsequent incubus at night and a reminder that once again they will have to face the army chasing them with guns and snapping at their heels in the morning. They also witnessed their older relatives being beaten up and bleeding. The cumulative effects on the tender minds can be devastating. Young boys have grown up with mental stresses weighing upon them and have taken up the gun as a natural recourse. Physical and sexual assaults on women as young as ten left a whole community with mental problems. These experiences in the formative years have cultivated a subculture of burgeoning hardened youngsters.

The tribes invading Kashmir from Aryan times did not show any respect for the natives of the paradise. Over the generations a dread was lurking in the depths of people's subconscious minds that an atrocity was imminent. They were nondescript as citizens and frustrated because their skills in handicrafts and art were not appreciated.

Some European travellers in the last century have filtered through Kashmir and made wild remarks about the people, without knowing what conditions they were going through with the repressive regimes. "They are intelligent! But they are devious, cunning and cowards," was one remark. It was unfortunate that the writers did not live within the fabric of the society for a long enough time, nor experience the burden of repression and the effect it had on their mental states. People live together and there is an intimate tenet of human bondage between them which makes their coveted society full of emotions, love and humour. People cry with trivial emotion. They weep, beat their chests, scream out loud in order to express anguish openly. The recent times have provided them with enough reasons to do just that! A symbolic story to tell would be the killing of a ten year old boy by Indian security forces in Srinagar. A reporter carrying a video camera arrived on the scene. A crying woman was seen running towards the pool of blood on the road. The blood, she was told, was from the dead body of her ten year old son, taken away to hospital by people. She instantly threw herself on the road, and smeared her face with the blood from her son's body and cried very loudly, beating her chest: "You murderers, you infidels, you cowards! What had my little boy done to you? You will pay for this!" She was shouting with fervour and distress.

Hari Singh, the Maharaja of Kashmir, was the second richest ruler in the subcontinent (first was the Nizam of Hydrabad). His people on the other hand were destitute and foraging for crumbs. He squandered money in London and Paris hotels on prostitutes. He played polo and enjoyed all the sporting luxuries the beautiful Valley of Kashmir can offer and yet people continued to live in their world of suffering.

In *1947* the British occupation of India ended at the same time as the occupation of Kashmir began. A new puppet government was installed by India in Kashmir... The agony and suffering for the people did not end and the 'Buffeted Baby Syndrome' remained unabated. I named it so because Kashmiris are babies! No one would dare invade Kashmir if Pathans lived here. Whatever else they do with their lives the Pathans kill first and ask questions later. Violence has never been a virtue with the people of Kashmir.

Torture was now inflicted on Kashmiris by people from their own community. I was the medical officer of the Central Jail in Srinagar. I witnessed innocent people being mauled by the dreaded policeman, called Qadir Ganderbali. Political or not, anyone who came under his paws was labelled as a Pakistani agent and beaten up. I know of Amin Siddiqi Turki from my neighbourhood who was repeatedly tortured. The torture started by stubbing out lit cigarettes on his body. He was then jumped upon and slashed with a knife. His testicles were pulled and he was hung upside down. Killings on the road continued and demonstrators were chased with live bullets being fired at them. The only reason for a supposedly Kashmiri ruler to behave like this towards his own people, was to demonstrate his allegiance to the supreme rulers in Delhi. A few more Kashmiris killed and a nod of approval would come accompanied with money and a bit extra to purchase more thugs in order to torture more people. People have a vivid memory of these events.

Harsh winters added to the maltreatment from a hostile government; people had no option but to migrate. In Indian cities a Kashmiri villager with no knowledge of the Indian language and wearing a Kashmiri cap was often an object of ridicule. He was called 'Hatho' and given very menial jobs for very little money. The trend to talk down to Kashmiris persisted when Indians came as visitors into Kashmir. A Kashmiri was a tribal native and was given no respect. A porter would have to give a piggy back ride to a fourteen-stone invalid Indian and take him to the hills for some scenery or a pilgrimage. He would be rewarded with a few paltry rupees and usually a lot of abuse with it.

I recall a trivial incident. We went with a small party of friends on a fishing day out and stayed the night in the forest hut overlooking the stream. One of the friends in the party was the son of an ex-Maharaja of an Indian state. We sat outside and were instantly surrounded by local people. "Send them away. I can't stand them surrounding us," the ex-prince said to an employee, pointing to the people. The words of the visitor stung me poignantly. I insisted they all stayed and chatted to them in Kashmiri, while others in the party went chasing the trout. I enjoyed the company of the locals and I thought the defiance to the attitude of the visitor, 'I like your country but I don't like you!' was justified

The influx of an army in Jammu and Kashmir and the space occupied by them has changed every aspect of life in all parts of the state. I will relate my personal experience to epitomise the deleterious effects of the mere presence of enormous numbers of armed forces dotted everywhere in Kashmir.

Gurez is the most beautiful valley in Kashmir, surrounded by 12,000 foot high mountains and a stream gushing down: clear blue waters, bisecting the basin and teeming with rainbow trout. Flocks of flying ducks are perched within sight of the stream. This place was like the Garden of Eden as described in the holy books! The Haba Khatoon and Razdani mountains overlook a row of villages comprising log cabins where the animals live below and within sight of the people living above. Not one nail had been used to erect these houses and the thatched roofs were perched over them in order to shield the life within from snow and storm. People had to dig their way into or out of their homes through the snow in winter. The mountains were carpeted with pines and cedars and lush green meadows bustled with wild flowers and animals. The air was so crisp, clear and cool, you could not breathe enough of this exhilarating aroma.

The people were a part of this paradise. They were gregarious and inherently happy. This was 1958. I was the only doctor within forty miles of Dawar, the main village, and I treated people, from dental extractions to delivering babies. The most astounding facts came to light during my tenure of service there. These people had never suffered from tuberculosis, venereal diseases, parasitic or viral diseases until 1947 when the Indian army entrenched in their hills. Suddenly, the whole population were caught as a virgin soil is for all the killer bugs you can think of. They had never been vaccinated. They dropped dead like flies. Women came out worse due to the stresses of pregnancy and sexual exploitation by the army. Men patients attending the hospital introduced their fifth wife to me. "What happened to others?" I asked. "They all died," was the answer. The army employed them for portage and it was an easy introduction to killer bugs. Money was a commodity rarely seen with any of the natives. Every item was bought and sold by the barter system. Money crept in, followed by abuse and devastation of these beautiful people.

My first job was to bring teams of vaccinators and extra supplies of medicines from Srinagar. I witnessed the scourge of civilisation creeping into this country. They were better off landlocked, happy and content, minding their lives in their primitive ways. Alongside this pestilence, people also witnessed their wild animals, especially the jungle goat, vanish and fish stocks in the streams going down. Both were consumed for food by the resident army.

The real panoply of tortures in the life history of the people in Kashmir only started when the Indian armed police were out in the streets of the villages and towns of Kashmir. The army assigned nomenclature to various types of torture. They were proud of the success in executing these novel forms of torture. The 'Operation

Shiva' meant the flaying of the body until it dismembered. 'Operation Tiger' was aimed at killing by 'slashing with a knife, a little at a time'. Bleeding profusely, and shock from pain would help to bring an end to another human being. The victim was coerced to talk part of the way to his death.

Rolling over victims with a road roller is the first time ever such a method of torture was practised in Kashmir. In interrogation centres, the victim is laid flat on hard ground, and a road roller run over his body. The muscles and bones get crushed and if they survived the ordeal and came as far the hospital they ended up with kidney failure due to the breakdown products of crushed muscles blocking the kidney tubules. They needed renal dialysis in hospitals and mostly died.

Bladder Bursting is one more experiment tried on the Kashmiris. The prisoner is made to drink gallons of water. The penis is tied with a string so they cannot void urine. Meanwhile the interrogation starts and if answers are not forthcoming, the experiment will continue. The swollen bladder becomes more painful. The military will then jump on his abdomen until the bladder will rupture inside, causing internal bleeding. The few survivors have related the story.

Hanging Upside Down with the feet tied to the ceiling has caused gangrene of the feet due to the tightening of the ropes and blindness due to prolonged hanging upside down.

Electrical Shocks and Burns with cigarette ends have left marks on the bodies of victims. These documented cases with photographs have been published by Human Rights organisations. Amnesty International have just published case histories of a new form of torture. (Index: ASA 20/33/95). The Indian army make captured young Kashmiris stand with bare feet in snow for many hours. Gangrene sets in and these people have had their feet amputated.

The army use every possible method to demean ordinary innocent citizens. The examples are simply abominable. They make people urinate and drink it. Women are grabbed by their hair and made to strip in front of their family and then are raped, a blow to a stringent moral and religious society. The army invade an estate and search every house, not just the one house suspected of harbouring a militant. Everyone in the area has to come out on the street: the elderly, children or the sick or handicapped. They never have a search warrant, and usually make their entry with their boots. They line up everyone and pick young men up and bundle them into trucks. Most of them are never seen again. That is why the relatives make a commotion at the time of their arrest. Bodies have been recovered from rivers, some of them are dismembered and dumped on main roads.

Kashmir has become a human abattoir, and its people are further decimated every day, creating a state of mayhem. *"When will it end?"* they ask.

Begam Akbar Jehan Abdullah, member of the Indian Parliament and wife of Sheikh Abdullah, called on prime minister Narasima Rad in August, 1993, and demanded an end to the killings in Kashmir. "Human Rights abusees tarnished the fair name of India. The policy of repression is undefensible and counterproductive, fanning hatred against India," Begam stated in categorical terms.

Haunted Children

"The child's one chance to grow properly in mind and body should be shielded from the mistakes, misfortunes and malignancies of the adult world. This protection should have the first call on society's concerns." This was from the Progress of Nations report by UNICEF. The parent world body UN has a covenant signed by all its members. It says, "Mankind owes to the child the best it has to give". In Kashmir schoolchildren talk about bombs and guns and have played with empty bullet shells for the last five years. Every child, no matter how old he or she is, has either witnessed a relative being beaten up or killed. Children of Kashmir experience fearsome nightmares at night: fleeing from an alien military, who snap at their heels all day long. In just one incident army trucks arrived at great speed through the narrow shopping street of Ishbar Nishat Kashmir on November 16th, 1992. Seven school children were killed when the army opened fire on a group of people standing in a shop minding their own business. Mushtaq, Mohammed and Tariq were only eight years old. An update of human rights abuses as on June 1st, 1994, makes gruesome reading. Some figures (Valley Reporter) shown are, 39,500 killed by indiscriminate firing on demonstrators, 358 burnt alive inside houses torched by the army, 23,558 people have been disabled for life and 225 children are recovering from broken bones.

287 youths were found in the River Jhelum with evidence of being drowned with their hands tied behind their backs in case they succeed in struggling back to the surface while still alive. About 50,000 people have disappeared either languishing in Indian jails, or on the run as fugitives, escaped into hiding or have emigrated. The list goes on and numbers are being added every day. Women have been molested, beaten up and raped.

In the squalid suburb of Chanapora, there is a strange lull following the crying and breast beating which came after their ordeal. On March 8th, International Woman's Day, a truck-load of the Central Reserve Police Force (CRPF) descended upon a group of houses, looted all the money, smashed televisions and radio sets and raped eight women. The army raid any built-up area, unleash destruction, and pursue a scorched earth policy as they leave the area.

One or two quotes from thousands in circulation may suffice to epitomise the extent of the atrocities committed and the mayhem the people of Kashmir find themselves in. McGirk reports in *The Independent,* March 19th, 1991: "800 soldiers raping about 60 women in February, 91." Tony Allen Mills reports in *The Sunday Times,* June 2nd, 91: "Delhi's sledgehammer turns paradise into hell."

Even as I am writing, there have been reports of eight people killed today. The spectre of violence goes on while the sanctimonious politicians confer, prevaricating the real issue in favour of their own political motives. The people of Kashmir are torn between tyranny and freedom and they fight on regardless of the stoical attitude of the outside world.

Natural Calamities

The population of Kashmir has received a setback over the years. The estimated population, including those who live outside Kashmir, is about fourteen million. The reduction in the population has been remarkable.

(i)   The 1877 Famine and consequent exodus took a huge toll. People died of starvation, or they were killed by the Dogra army to stop them fleeing. Thousands settled in India and some found refuge in other parts of the world. There were no food granaries to tide them over during the crisis.

(ii) The awful dispensation by earthquakes, pestilence, repression, medical ignorance, epidemics like cholera, the plague, tuberculosis and viral diseases reduced the population. None of the preventive medical measures were practised until the World Health Organisation and UNICEF undertook the job.

(iii) The effect of the Indian army living in far-flung areas of the Himalayan territory and introducing venereal disease and communicable bacterial diseases has caused epidemics of grave proportions. Tuberculosis was unknown in some isolated regions. They were caught in a virgin soil state without any body defences.

(iv) Political killings have taken a very big toll of the human population in Kashmir. Kashmiris have been ruled with a gun facing them at every corner. The mass massacres by the Indian army at fourteen different places filled all the martyrs' graveyards. The memories of the Amritsar Jalianwala Bagh and Mylae massacres by the British were rekindled with more intensity. One incident will exemplify the state of the human abattoir that Kashmir has become. The Indo-Tibetan force of the Indian army were travelling in an ambulance van near Islamia college campus when they heard students shouting slogans. They were demonstrating against their university. The army opened fire on the students and sprayed them with bullets, killing more than a hundred. This demonstration was not even political. An investigation was ordered by the Indian government to appease the media. No results ever came out.

In May 1966, the Indian government subjected the people of Kashmir to an ordeal of dragging them to the polling booths by coercion. The elections were held to get representatives for the Indian parliament. The world press witnessed the drama of the army performing an unusual role of pulling people out of their homes to cast votes! "Indian guns force Kashmir voters to the ballot box," was the main news in *The Times* on May 24th, 1966. All the major dailies carried the news. This atrocity of 'phantom democracy' was repeated in September 1996. Some fear-stricken members of the public lined up to vote, an easier way to survive. There is a limit to the abuse of power and dehumanising a whole nation.

In conclusion, it can safely be said that the people of Kashmir had their share of suffering, either from the repressive regimes or unfortunate circumstances.

You cannot draw up an indictment against a whole people. The use of force alone is but temporary. It may subside insurrection for a moment, but it does not remove the necessity of subduing again. A nation is not governed which is perpetually to be conquered. A lesson to learn for the occupation forces.

'So far and no more' is a popular slogan. It may be a far cry, but people are resigned to continuing their struggles, no matter what it takes or how long it takes. 'Freedom' has become axiomatic to survival. No other nation in the world has endured suffering over so many years as the people of Kashmir.

GENESIS AND GENES

Anthropology of a Kashmiri

The people of Kashmir are comfortable living as a gregarious race and wary of external influences on their civilisation. They find it difficult to totally blend in with other communities of the subcontinent. They like to think they are a separate breed, having in their origins a conglomeration of various cultures from the past. Kashmir is a meeting point of three empires, Russia, China and South Asia. There are three languages: Dardic and Kashmiri, Indo-European and Tibeto-Mongolian. There are three religions dominant in the state, Hinduism, Buddhism and Islam. Each one left a gamut of indelible characteristics in the culture of the society, passed down from generation to generation.

Kashmiri skin has a light complexion. Their eyes are dark brown and cheekbones raised. The anthropologist would say that these characteristics were Greek in origin. Alexander of Macedonia in 326 BC, came like a whirlwind through Kashmir. He left a big contingent of soldiers behind. They stayed and lived their lives to pass on the progeny. Hellenic sculptures and Greek architecture in ancient properties remain as evidence.

A Kashmiri by birth has the genetic configuration of a mixture of characteristics from central Asia, Mongolia, Greece, Persia, and India. The tell-tale signs from each civilisation are evident in varying degrees.

There is evidence that Kashmiris are genetically an intelligent race. The depth of intelligence harbours creativity and a myriad of original features. Like other humans, they have frivolous moments but if opportunities are afforded, they prove their excellence and acumen. They make good scholars, and scientists. They are the best craftsmen known in the world today. It is because the society is composted and has imbibed a wide spectrum of outside influences, and there are communities who differ from each other, especially from towns to urban areas.

In 1665, Francois Bernier was one of the first European travellers visiting Kashmir. The French doctor attached to Delhi Royal Court made his journey with Emperor Akban's entourage. He wrote that: "Kashmir was famed as Paradise of the Indies. People are far superior in culture and talent to everyone else in the subcontinent." (Francis Brunel, *Kashmir*, Calcutta, Rupta.)

Sir Francis Younghusband; a British resident in Kashmir (1903), explorer of the Himalayas, a mystic and founder of the 'World Congress of Faiths', observed, that a Kashmiri soldier is a contradiction in terms but their good points are that they are intelligent and can turn their hand to most things.

A Kashmiri wears an affable expression and has a simplistic mind. That is why they are gullible and look innocent, sometimes to their detriment. They had blind faith in their leader Sheikh Abdullah. In an esoteric frenzy they even found his name inscribed in the leaves of trees. Sheikh Abdullah, a schoolteacher, emerged as a leader at a time when people were suffering the effects of enforced slavery from a cruel despotic ruler. They were reduced to a nondescript identity and deprived of adult suffrage. This background made them vulnerable. They perceived a glimmer of hope in their leader. They listened to him, followed him and died for him. It comes as no surprise that the whole nation was devastated when their stalwart leader was duped.

A Kashmiri is peace-loving by nature. He will endure any hardship to be left in peace and, given a chance, snuggle up to a *kangri* (fire pot) for warmth and comfort and be a fainéant lounger. A British old lady, on a coffee morning, said to her friends: "I felt compassion for this poor man. He was sweating profusely, laid down on the grass with the scorching sun blazing down on him. I asked him, 'Why not sleep under the shade of the chinar tree, just a few yards away?' It is much cooler!"

"Thank you Madam," he replied, eagerly sitting up. "I will go and lie under the tree, as you say. How much will you pay me?" A little story which epitomises further connotations. The personality of a typical Kashmiri man who suffered abject poverty is bereft of enthusiasm and has a mindset of subservience and humility.

Lord Birdwood (1832-1917, an Anglo-Indian doctor and writer on India), remarked in his chronicles that a Kashmiri will suffer and endure but he will not fight. "I have watched a couple hurling insults at each other, perspiration standing out on their brows, their raised fists clenched for the first blow; but it never falls!"

The people of Kashmir can also be temperamental and lash out with great ferocity. The emotion does not last for long, and they revert back to a sedate demeanour quickly. Kashmiris have been known to be 'Zulum Parast' (worshippers of tyranny). By and large they are not vindictive and the storm of temper will mellow and melt down, like fizz from a bottle of pop.

Kashmiris by nature are altruistic and tolerant. The complex genetic background is responsible for the high level of inter-faith tolerance and their living in harmony. As a tourist-oriented nation they love foreigners. The people of Kashmir are known for their hospitality. There are no recorded incidents of violent xenophobic activity. In demonstrations against the 'theft of the sacred relic' episode in 1965, the whole society across the board rallied together, and mobilised their resources. Roadside soup kitchens, free distribution of food and clothing for people were organised on a grand scale. During any adversity like curfews imposed by the military or celebrations on a happy occasion, no one is left on their own.

Kashmir is known for its lively parties. They are arranged at the slightest excuse. The first haircut of a baby or an ear piercing ceremony for a little girl, or the circumcision of a baby boy, becomes a big occasion, and celebrations follow. Marriages are celebrated for seven days on the trot! Even a death becomes an occasion for special meals to be prepared by friends and relatives to feed the bereaved family and the rest of the community for many days. The people crave to live in a happy and peaceful world. Peace is integral to their existence.

Kashmiris have a distinct habitat. In urban areas they live in a cluster of small houses made from unburnt brick set in wooden frames of cedar, fir or pine with pointed roofs. A typical scene of a Kashmir village is set in the middle of vast fields with a few small shops selling essential goods and services. The roofs are made from earth, affording a high degree of insulation from cold and trapping the heat inside. These roofs also provided an allotment for a luscious growth of vegetables. In Gurez houses were made with a tongue in groove technique with no nails used in the construction process. Men in Gurez did all the knitting of woollen garments with wooden needles, while women worked in the fields. The mobile central heating earthenware pot with burning coal called 'Kangri' is tucked underneath long robes and will accompany them wherever they go.

The staple diet for a Kashmiri is rice with vegetables and, if and when affordable, meat. Meat is eaten by all, irrespective of religion or caste. Brahmin Hindus in India are strict practising vegetarians. Brahmins in Kashmir eat meat. Harisa is a special recipe only found in Kashmir. The name Harisa is known in Iran and Turkey, but the recipes are different. Harisa is prepared in a makeshift oven from rice or flour, lamb and a variety of spices. The process involves an overnight mashing of the mixture by hand and making this pasty semi-liquidated concoction and sizzling it with hot oil as it is served. A sumptuous breakfast only eaten occasionally, especially on frosty and bitterly cold mornings.

The people in Kashmir say they can live on fresh air and music. The local folk enjoy classical Sufi music and instrumental music is the soul of the society. There is subtle depth in the meaning of the Sufi verses which make them almost divine. Kashmiris sit through nights listening to music and songs.

Kashmiris have demonstrated a marathon endurance for work. They can sit at a carpet or a shawl for six months at a time, fifteen hours a day, every day, and take pride in the masterpiece they produce. The physical stamina is remarkable when Kashmiri porters carry overweight handicapped tourists on their backs trekking through the mountains for sightseeing or pilgrimages to shrines. The mosaic of the personality of a Kashmiri is stupendous and unique!

Sense of Humour!

The only offset to unhappiness is happiness, so it was some divine law of compensation that gave Kashmiris the ability to squeeze humour out of an existence from which they could extract little else.

The dominant feature in the personality of a Kashmiri is an ambivalence of emotions and sense of humour. They pull humour out of calamities. Comical quips are made from names of people and the behaviour of both themselves and outsiders. Practical jokes are also common. Poems are made from funny incidents or sometimes serious situations.

They offer prevarication as a spiced dish! It is not that lies are spoken with harm in mind, but they thrive on a whiff of humour. Some incidents are worthy of mention.

During the early Dogra rule, an English revenue officer was camped in a village, sorting out problems for the locals. One applicant, a Kashmiri Pandit was sent away, having faked his complaint for compensation. Early next morning, the officer opened his front door, only to find the Pandit standing on his head, refusing to move until his demands were met. "He has been like that since last night," the officer was told by his servant. The Pandit was ordered to be turned the right way up at once and his request was granted!

Bawling and screaming, a man arrived complaining of an assault on him. He brought a lock of hair carefully wrapped in paper as evidence. It was horsehair!

With a Holy Book held close to his chest a man took this oath: "I swear by this life (pointing to his chest) I speak the truth. The Holy Book is my witness." It transpired that a frog was hidden under the clothes. "This life" was meant for the frog!

Walter Lawrence had an experience with a Kashmiri Pandit. The little man presented written petitions three times before the commissioner which were found untrue and promptly rejected. He was warned that another petition and he would be reported to the local police. Next day, the Pandit appeared again with a paper in his hand. He was ordered to be thrown out at once. The Pandit pleaded that the paper was not a petition but a 'poem' that he wished to present. The poem recited his grievances!

A Kashmiri would do anything to get sympathy but keeps his humour alive. He would smear grey mud from the rice fields on his face, or hang a rope made from rice straw round his neck, with a brick as a pendant. The brick signified that he has been reduced to the condition of a clod, and the rice straw, that his wife has destroyed him!

Recently, Indian army officers looking for militants, grabbed a little boy of nine. He was ordered to give information. "Sir, I will take you to the area commander, follow me!" Meandering through narrow alleys and climbing a few walls for a mile or so he stopped and knocked on a door. The soldiers took position, guns pointing. The door was answered by a seven year old boy wearing a barrette cap. "That is *him*! He is the most dreaded commander we have!" exclaimed the little informer. "Get him." Both boys got a beating before being released.

A man arrived to see the revenue commissioner completely nude! He said his uncle had turned him naked into the world. It was cold and the commissioner offered him an old suit to wear. Next day the uncle came with signs of castigation hoping to receive something similar.

The pertinacious nature of a Kashmiri is also laudable. My father employed a young man from the Tral village to work as a salesman in his Connaught Place shop. A Scandinavian tourist strolled past the shop and browsed in, showing a casual interest in the furs. The salesman followed him with a bundle of fur coats and went to his hotel room. "No, I want no furs, get out," was the answer. The door was shut in his face. The night passed. Next morning, the tourist found the salesman sleeping outside his bedroom door with his fur coats. "Sir, I am sorry I had to be such a nuisance. I must sell you a fur coat." One was sold!

Everybody gets a nickname. Physical attributes or cruel handicaps become the ingredients of a name. No one is spared! Prominent leaders are called 'Humps', 'Bent fingers', 'Lanky', 'Dandy', 'Nosy', 'Butch', or whatever, and the people recognise the names. Poems are made from funny incidents or sometimes serious situations.

Human Bondage

A family in Kashmir is one unit. They live together. They share everything – emotions, love, care, and understanding for each other's problems. You only need to overhear the loud wailing in shrines. It is heart-rending when the women mention the names of children, grandchildren or even others not directly related, giving details of their suffering, as if before a doctor, and ask God to help them, give them the best of health and pockets full of money. This bond is highly rated. Walter Lawrence writes: "I have often come across a woman in some deserted spot singing and wailing for a husband dead long since!"

A piece of bread brought home must be shared by everyone.

Religion and the Aura of Sanctity

Kashmir is studded with Muslim shrines, Buddhist temples and is a home to Hindu gods. It is the haven for Sufism, a hermitage for the great saints and the birthplace for the legends of history. There are hallmarks of a presence from all the prophets and visitations from God. Kashmir has been compared to the Garden of Eden with the luscious green atmosphere, delicious apples and beautiful meandering white streams.

The cadence of their lifestyle, the nimble personality and milieu of spirituality pervading their lives, characterises a Kashmiri quite distinctly from everyone else in the subcontinent of South Asia.

AURA OF SANCTITY

Is Kashmir a Divine Place?

The sacred mountains of the Himalayas are a home for the angels who have descended upon earth and for the saints who spent their lives in thought and prayer. History and legend support this view.

People in Kashmir from all faiths are believers in God and the aura of sanctity dominates their lives. There are a handful of recent atheists. They are insignificant. Every sacred place is very dear to the people and a source of supreme felicity. Shrines with relevance to all religions have been desecrated over the years. The spiritual powers dominating the atmosphere in these holy mountains can only be felt as an experience. That is why people in Kashmir consider their country a 'sanctuary' where God has a direct impact on their lives.

Kashmir is tucked away in the foothills of the most magnificent mountains of the world and clad with the most luscious growth of trees, vegetation and flora which provide an ideal ambience for divinity. You only need to wander out into the hills, and the feeling of God's presence gets hold of every fibre of your body. The huge expanse of still and motionless parts of nature will provide an eerie experience for a person new to the area.

Legend has it that Adam was dropped into Kashmir from the Garden of Eden. He brought the apple stolen from Heaven with him. That started the growth of masses of apple trees still abundant in Kashmir!

The most venerated of shrines for the Hindus are Martand, the Amarnath and the Vishnu Devi. Jammu is called the Temple City.

Martand. The sun temple was built about two thousand years ago by the Kashmiri King Lalityaditya Mukhtapida. The temple has, over the years, been vandalised.

Temples of Avantipur. The ruins are reminiscent of the ninth century architecture of high calibre. The temples dedicated to Vishnu and Shiva were built by King Avantivarman. The place derives its name from him.

Amarnath Caves. A regular place for pilgrimages, the caves house an icicle which denotes the Lingham (a sacred phallic symbol), and is revered by many people of Hindu faith to Lord Shiva and Parvati, (Hindu Gods).

Kalishri is a temple beside the holy shrine of Shah Hamadan. Both Muslims and Hindus visit and pray side by side. Hindus call Shah Hamadan, the Muslim saint, 'Kahanoi' who is very much revered by them as well as by the Muslims. All the Sufi saints like Sheikh Nur-ud-Din, Bulbul Shah and Syed Yaqub Sarfi have a great place of honour for both Hindus as well as Muslims. 'Kashmiriat' has been claimed to be a blend of allegiance to Sufism in Kashmir.

One tradition in Kashmir stands out as remarkable: the morning walk to the shrines. Hindus of all ages are seen at the break of dawn walking to the shrines, with their heads completely covered, chanting sermons, wherever they are in Kashmir. Muslims likewise take their morning walks for miles on end to their chosen shrine or on special days to visit a particular shrine in order to reach it before the dawn breaks.

The special places of pilgrimage for the Hindus are the Amar Nath caves. The Martand and Avantipora temples unfortunately are occupied by the army these days. The Vishnu Devi, forty miles from Jammu, is another pilgrimage centre visited by many thousands of Hindus from all over India. The Raghunath temple, known to worshippers as a place of worship to Lord Rama, is the best known. The temple is full of artistic features and is covered with gold on three walls.

Hindus of Kashmir not only pray to Vishnu Devi, Ragya Khsgeer Bhawani, Sharika, Shiva and Parvati but also propound the Shaivite doctrine of 'Trika', a philosophy of recognition, and abstinence from material comforts.

Every religion over the years has provided a hypothesis of its own. There are legendary tales about the origins of this country.

Millions of years back, Kashmir was an expanse of water, like a gigantic lake. The water then drained away through outlets now called rivers, and Kashmir emerged as mountains, valleys and lakes. The different versions of its creation can be described in a compendious way.

King Solomon employed an ingenious method of canalisation to drain the lake according to some writers. Human labour was employed. The rivers were created, surfacing earth for people to inhabit.

Satisar (The Big Lake) inhabited by snakes according to Hindu mythology, was drained by Lord Shiva (Hindu God) by making a crater in the mountains with a hard blow from the weapon he carried. Water, having been drained through an outlet of the Baramulla gorge, left lakes and land for people to live on. After creating Kashmir, Rishi Kashyap left his people the land and River Vitasta to live on. The name Kashmir was derived from Kashyap, according to the writers of the chronicles about this era.

The more sceptical believe that there was a volcanic eruption forming the crater in Baramulla. This theory has geological evidence in the substrata near the mountains. Kashmir is in the volcanic zone of the earth. Earthquakes in the past have caused great devastation.

Moses led his people to Kashmir from Egypt. As proof of this theory the elders in Kashmir even today get called 'Joo' after their name derived from the word Jew, as a mark of respect. Scholars in ancient history have stated that the first inhabitants of Kashmir came from a tribe B'nai Israil. They were Jews and migrated with their leader Moses and settled in Kashmir. It is believed by some theologians that Moses is buried in Kashmir. Even today in Bandipur Kashmir, a grave is present on the peak of the hill called 'Baal Bebu'. The name mentioned in the Old Testament as 'Mount Nebo'. Maybe for that reason alone Jews of the world should have empathised with the people of Kashmir and their plight!

Jesus Christ is believed to be buried in Kashmir. The place called Rosabal, near Khanyar Srinagar, is venerated and visited by thousands of Muslims, as the last resting place of Jesus Christ. There are footprints and a tomb representing the place where the burial took place. Jesus was taken down from the crucifix, he then came back to life and was helped to emigrate away from his assassins. He eventually ended up in Kashmir, lived up to an old age (120 years) and died. This theory has been reinforced in a varied form by the German theologian, Holger Kerstern. He says that the three Wise Men were, in fact, Buddhist monks from Kashmir who set out to seek reincarnation of their spiritual master who for them turned out to be Jesus. People believe the millennium will begin in Kashmir; they have the spiritual background with all their sacrifices for ultimate salvation.

The Jesus' emigration theory has been investigated with inconclusive results.

The fact remains that all religions of the world have a stake in Kashmir. It is easy to understand why even trying to violate its physical boundaries will bring doom and disaster to the invaders. History has shown this to be true. Mongols, Afghans, Sikhs and even the Dogra dynasty burnt their hands badly with their meddling into the hotbed of sacrosanct Kashmir. Akbar with his massive force entered Kashmir on *June 5th, 1589*. It was not long after that, that lightening struck Lahore, causing a devastating fire and melted all Abkar's gold and silk so that the melted gold was flowing through the streets of Lahore!

Zulfi Khan, a descendant of Ghengis Khan, violated Kashmir and perished in a blizzard along with his loot and many thousands of slaves, crossing the Devasar Pass on his way back to Mongolia. The Afghan governor, having committed atrocities in Kashmir, was killed by his own brother, fighting for the throne after Abdali. Ranjit Singh, the Sikh who plundered the sanctity of Kashmir, died after a miserable defeat in his war with the British. The Dogra dynasty ended after a long trail of crimes with Hari Singh abdicating in disgrace and disappearing into exile. It remains to be seen what the future holds for all friends and foes of Kashmir. It may sound esoteric, but people in Kashmir believe in the punishments from God. They take an adverse prayer or a curse very seriously. An argument between two people for instance, may end in a loud 'ill-wishing prayer' or a curse. That is reciprocated. It worries them in case the 'prayer' has invoked Providence and will happen in reality, more than the pain from the physical blows which rarely fall!

Jammu and Kashmir are studded with shrines and sacred places. Sufism originated in Kashmir. It has one ideology where all religions join along a single path, altruism, abstinence from instinctual desires and avarice. The great saints of Kashmir have left behind a treasure of knowledge into depths of theology and Sufism. The fourteenth century shrine housing the great saint Sheikh Nur-ud-Din Wali was burnt to the ground in a recent chase for militants by the Indian army. Sheikh Nur-ud-Din Wali was also known as Nund Rishi and is venerated by the Hindus of Kashmir as well as by Muslims. He was born in 1377 and was the founder of the Richi cult in Sufism. The tenets of his teachings were austerity, penance and abstinence from greed, rich non-vegetarian food and avarice. The time of penance would include celibacy. He and his ninety-nine disciples, called Khalifas, have a shrine in every part of Kashmir. They worshipped God and spent all their time preaching the virtues of humanity, tolerance and help for the needy. Shrines have become places of worship as well as venues for imparting spiritual education and the virtues of altruism. People share food and money during times of crisis.

The Hazratbal shrine is where the Holy Hair of Prophet Mohomed is kept. Other shrines of great importance to all Kashmiris are Hazrat Dastigir, Makhdoom Sahib, Ziyarat Buibul Shah, and Shahi Hamadan mosque which houses the tomb of Mir Syed Ali Hamadani. Mir Syed came from Hamadam, Persia and preached Islam and tolerance for all communities. For Hindus he was the 'Kahnoi', and Muslims throng to the place as their Khanikah moula (a place of God).

Ladakh is a haven for monasteries and statues of Buddha, a testimony of the great Buddhist civilisation. Hemis is the prime monastery and the festival marking the birth of Padmasambhava is celebrated with drums and pipes by Lamas and locals alike. Buddhism has made an indelible mark on the societies of Asia and the Far East from the days of Ashoka who was a ruler in Kashmir and had other parts of Asia under his domain. In 260 BC, Buddhism spread throughout the continent of Asia merging with the Veda to evolve Shaivism.

People of all faiths have a special relationship with God in whichever form they pray to Him. They associate their prayers with the place they live in. Kashmiris have remarked on numerous occasions that during the time they lived outside Kashmir they have been alienated from God and have felt unhappy.

'We will strive to keep the integrity of our spiritual haven, even if that means death for us.' You get that message from the grass roots and every section of the society.

Events With Poignant Memories for the People of Kashmir

December 27th, 1963: a devastating sacrilege was committed. The 27th is an inauspicious date for Kashmir. It was a bleak and chilly evening of that December when the Holy Hair of Prophet Mohammed (Peace be upon him) was stolen from the Hazratbal Shrine. (The other significant 27th of course was the day when armies entered Kashmir in 1947).

Haji Mohammed Khalil Gania was one of the trustees of the relic and that morning he found that the place had been rummaged through and the relic was missing. The six million people of Kashmir, including the non-Muslims, were out on the roads demonstrating in protest and mourning the loss. Nowhere in the world is a recorded example of the solidarity shown between all inhabitants remonstrating in the way the people of Kashmir did. The whole population was out on the roads. Food was donated in abundance and roadside soup kitchens were established. Many thousands of demonstrators stopped for a break as they marched on. Homes were deserted, schools were closed and transport came to a standstill. The relic was eventually restored but the event was shrouded in the mystery of who stole it or what was the motive behind this act of blasphemy? The world realised the degree of faith which binds the people of Kashmir together.

The Holy Hair from the beard of the Prophet Mohammed was in Medina up to 1634. It was kept by Sayid Abdullah, a devotee. He also had the saddle and turban belonging to Hazrat Ali, the son-in-law of the Prophet and the fourth Caliph of Islam. Abdullah was banished by the incumbent Caliph of Medina. He left Medina carrying with him the treasures. He arrived in India two years later, and Shah Jehan the Mogul King impressed with his possessions settled him in Bijapur. Abdullah died after twenty-three years and his son Sayid Hamid inherited the treasures. Sayid Hamid having lost the support of feuding Moguls became destitute and poor. He accepted a favour of help from a Kashmiri trader, called Khwaja Nuruddin Ashawari. Ashawari wanted the treasures. Hamid refused but had a visit in his dream from Prophet Mohammed who asked him not to disappoint the trader and give him the relic. Ashawari set off for Kashmir, his homeland, along with his family and the relic but was intercepted as he passed through Lahore by Aurangzeb (The Mogul Emperor) who saw the treasure and said, "This supreme blessing ranks higher than all my domain, my throne, my crown, my faith and my world." He ordered the relic to be installed in Ajmir to the great grief of the people of Lahore, who wanted to keep it in Lahore. The relic was given a safe home in Ajmir Sherif's shrine. After nine days the King saw the Prophet in his dream. He was told to restore it back to Ashawari. Ashawari died before he got to Kashmir. He was taken to Kashmir along with the relic preserved in a sandalwood box. The relic was installed in the Bhagi Sadiq mosque which was afterwards named 'Hazratbal'. His wish to be buried near the relic was carried out. Ashawari was buried in the garden of the mosque. His daughter, Inayat Begam married Khwaja Balagi Bande. The Bande descendants have since been showing the relic to many thousands of believers on the holy days of the year.

Desecration of holy places by Indian armed forces, during their anti-militant operations, have left grievous wounds in the hearts of all Kashmiris which will take a long time to heal.

The *Hazratbal* shrine stands on the banks of Lake Dal and symbolises the magnitude of faith people have. The relic of the Holy Hair belonging to prophet Mohammed is housed inside. Thousands of people attend Friday prayers. The shrine was cordoned off by the Indian army in order to lay a siege on the worshippers inside. They sent soldiers inside to look for militants and built bunkers on the perimeter of the shrine in order to barricade it. These operations were an attempt to demonstrate to people that the power and muscle of militarism do not spare the holy places.

The tomb of the Great King or Badshah of Kashmir, known as Shahi Khan or Zain-ul-Abidin, whose golden rule lasted fifty years (1420-70). Three generations of my own family are also buried here.

The Palace of Fairies (Pari Mahal), school of spiritual learning, built by Dara Shikoh who was the son of emperor Shahjehan, on a mountain top overlooking Lake Dal.

The economy of Kashmir is self-sustainable.
Handmade silk carpets from Kashmir are unmatched by any others in the world. This carpet, in the family, is considered an investment item which will never depreciate in value. It is smooth in texture and superb in quality.

Houseboats for the tourists in the most beautiful setting in the world.

They want to create desolation and call it peace. As a first step towards achieving that end, they bomb-blast homes and shops, razing all property to the ground, along with the people in them.

This twenty year old has joined an estimated 40,000 other Kashmiris in martyrdom for the noble cause of freedom and justice for his nation.

1586 heralded an era of Mogul rule with architectural excellence and the construction of great monuments and gardens.

Gateway to the city of Nagar Nagar built by Akbar.

The stone mosque (Pathar Masjid) built by Nur Jehan, wife of Emperor Jehangir. The mosque stands majestically today in the heart of the city.

Smiling they may be, the 'Awesome Foursome' made millions cry.

(Top left)   Lord Louis Mountbatten, the last viceroy of India (1947).

(Top right)   Maharaja Hari Singh, the last of the Dogra rulers (1846 – 1947).

(Bottom left)   Sheikh Mohammed Abdullah, Prime Minister of Jammu and Kashmir (1947 – 1953).

(Bottom right) Pandit Jawaharlal Nehru, Prime Minister of India (1947 – 1964).

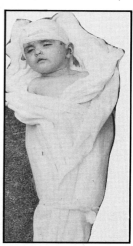

The child's one chance to grow properly in mind and body should be shielded from the mistakes, misfortunes and malignancies of the adult world. This protection should have the first call on society's concerns.

(Top)   A child in exile.

(Bottom left)   Baby with a broken arm.

(Bottom right)   Army bullet piercing the head.

Hazrat Dastighir in Khanyar is a very respected shrine. It was here that a mourning procession, carrying a coffin, was intercepted by the army. It was like Doomsday to witness the forces open fire on the coffin and the mourners. The army went inside the shrine with boots on in order to chase the fleeing people. Ten people were killed in the massacre and the dead bodies were riddled with bullets.

Chrar Sherif, the famous fourteenth century shrine of the great saint Sheikh Nur-ud-Din Wali was a symbol for peace and harmony. It is an irony of fate that its peaceful people should have suffered, their homes torched and the innocent civilians killed. On May 10th, 1995, the Chrar Sherif shrine, adjacent mosque and 2,200 houses and shops were torched by bombs dropped over their homes. This shrine was sacred to both Hindus and Muslims of Kashmir.

The *Khankah* Shrine of Hazrat Ali Hamadani has been violated on many occasions for searches and chasing militants.

There are a great number of mosques, Hindu temples and Sikh gurdwaras which have been burnt down, and blasphemed.

The hurt caused by these outrages against religious shrines will never be forgotten. The aura of spiritual ambience is not a sanctimonious display by worshippers but a true dogma which people of all faiths believe in and will die for. This phenomenon may not be explicable to other nations of the world. Kashmir will always be a closed parochial society with a commitment to the philosophy of Sufism and faith in God.

ECONOMY OF KASHMIR

A Fiscal Profile

Kashmir may not be a rich country and cannot afford to build skyscrapers and motorways but freedom fanatics deny that its survival is dependent upon external help. They are convinced that as a free nation, the people of Kashmir will bring out their best talents and create wealth. Democracy may be restored and make people feel like true citizens. The potential for growth could be endless.

Father Jerome Xavier, a priest, who accompanied Emperor Akbar and his massive invasion force into Kashmir in June 1589, wrote: "The Kingdom of Caximir (Kashmir) is one of the pleasantest and most beautiful countries to be found in the whole of the East. It is rich with natural beauty, pastures, orchards, gardens, waterways, countless springs, lakes and rivers but with the cruel irony that Kashmiri people are starving." The interminable political repression and odyssey of occupation which lasted until 1752 under the Moguls and then continued with Afghans, and Sikhs, never gave the people a chance to develop their economic base.

Akbar forced men to wear long feminine robes (Pharans) in order to kill their fighting instinct and ensure an obsequious populus which he could rule. The cruel irony is that these robes are now used to hide weapons by freedom fighters and have become the national dress.

Kashmir could be a utopia for the idealist and provide a comfortable living for her inhabitants. Nature's attributes make Kashmir a heaven upon earth! Believers say God was in His best leisurely disposition and frame of artistic imagination when He created Kashmir!

In 1835, the European traveller, Godfrey Vigne, describing the potential resourcefulness of Kashmir, said, "Given a chance to develop their skills in agriculture, industries and exploitation of mineral resources, Kashmir will be a miniature England in the heart of Asia."

Jammu, Kashmir, Ladakh, Gilgat and Baltistan, as one unit, worked together in the past as a melange of talents. The skills to expropriate the best of Nature's resources combined with the inherent excellence of the creative, artistic and industrial flair of the people, will restore a credible economic base. A feeling of confidence can pervade the society.

The question has often been asked whether or not Kashmir on its own will continue to have a servile economy and sooner or later fall into the lap of a sympathetic motherly country, on the premise that lessons must be learnt from the past when Kashmir was deliberately plunged into destitution due to nefarious intrigues. An instrument of subversion was to render people poor and break their morale, then offer them help with handouts, like cheap rice! (US aid PL40). People under obligation of this generosity would offer universal obeisance to authority.

The economy of Kashmir has been spiralling backwards with an erosion of its industrial base and its perpetual political upheavals. It was not more than five decades ago, even taking the repressive Dogra regime into account, that Kashmir was a land of plenty and people had more food than they could eat, more wool than they could use for their clothes and all the raw materials they needed for industry and handicrafts.

Kashmir was a big exporter of agricultural produce, horticulture, meat and poultry. Silk cloth was rolling out of sericulture mills, considered the best in the world for its texture and refinement. The abundance of forest and forest products made the economy of Kashmir the most viable in the subcontinent. Handicrafts, precious and semi-precious jewellery manufactured in Kashmir went very far into the world. Cashmere shawls became a status symbol for the aristocracy in Europe. Medicines and chemicals from indigenous plants used to be researched and manufactured in Kashmir. All these institutions have fallen into ruins.

It may be logical to make some observations to underpin the suspicion that industries were surreptitiously discouraged to exploit local assets. The power generator came to a halt, and the World Bank money to implement hydroelectric projects ebbed away. Tourism collapsed even before 1989. Tourists were given a raw deal, beauty spots were vandalised and the total infrastructure which Kashmir was proud of became disfigured.

Agriculture has retrogressed. Forests are denuded, threadbare. The best rainbow trout in the world were dynamited for food. Scab, a fungus, has been introduced into apple trees so that the famous Kashmir apples are now treated as second rate produce, in order to help Himachal Predesh orchards to thrive. There are other legitimate factors which are intrinsically responsible for the devastation of the economy in Kashmir:

1. Industries set up in recent years quickly closed down. The raw materials were sold off in Bombay for a quick profit. The carcasses of these industries are empty shells in ruins.

2. Foodstuffs including meat, groceries, chickens or even milk were imported from Punjab at cheap rates. Local production ceased.

3. Forest based industries already working with local raw materials were closed. Timber, pulp for making paper, a match factory, furniture or raw materials for any other forest based product were exported. Walnut wood, an important raw material for handicrafts, has been shipped out to Europe as 'logs'. The silk factories, woollen mills, leather processing factories, fur tanneries and drug research laboratories all using local materials were shut down.

4. Kashmir has been known for its fruit industry. The quality of all the fruit grown in the past has been exemplary. The setback to this thriving industry has been through a possible introduction of a fungal infestation and this scourge on the total multi-billion rupee fruit industry lasted many years. All canning and preservation units have over the years closed down.

5. The handicrafts industry was once the source of pride and prosperity for Kashmir. It was reduced to a cheap production line for a quick profit. All controls over the traditional acumen into quality were abolished or an imposition of regulations used for extracting bribes. The customers had also changed. The Indian visitors wanted cheap goods. Art elements and exclusive fabrics of craftsmanship disappeared. The youth living under the umbrella of this scale of corruption succumbed to the pressures and joined in to look for easy money. The skill element, the motivation and the economy as a whole was spiralling backwards and as demands to cash in on cheap prosperity imported from India increased, frustration crept in and winters of destitution deepened. People lost all interest and motivation. The vicious cycle of the demise of this industry was thus completed.

6. The supply side of the economy, eg education and training, have been completely in the hands of incumbent governing despots. Politicians themselves had uncertain futures and patriotic doctrines were remote in their minds. Methods adopted to train and supply skilled workers to the industry were related to what the rulers themselves could extract from such measures, either cash or a favour to a relative. This vicious cycle of exploitation resulted in the young people living in villages remaining unskilled and emigrating to the cities. A little cash stuck under their noses by the minority bourgeois class, easily lured them into menial jobs. They come to the cities at an impressionable age and become a prey to the prevailing evils creeping into the society. In the meantime, they are exposed to all perfidious methods of exploitation. The corrupt practices in the government ranks are passed down to people at the grass roots. A few privileged ones coddled and supported by the money of relatives in politics end up in technical colleges. The effects of these metamorphoses of their minds have altered the direction of the ingenuity which Kashmiris are famous for. The bright talent in young people remains repressed.

The people of Kashmir have special needs in education, health and social services. These may not apply and be practised elsewhere in the subcontinent. In education their need is to acquire environmental skills and training. Children will need to learn the cultural background and the essence of their heritage. Kashmiri and other local languages will need to be enhanced and put back on the social scene. Recent years have seen a remarkable erosion of languages. The whole curriculum will require a review. Social services resources in Kashmir have been despoiled. A craft shop started for making various goods closed as soon as the money dried up. In order to blend the talent available, with the need in the market place for manufactured goods, the ideas have to be indigenous. The depth of the cultural background and influx of civilisations from different parts of the world place the people of Kashmir in a distinct category. Elocution of local dialects and languages cannot be replicated by people born outside Kashmir.

People are brainwashed to accept corrupt practices. They learn about faking and deception. One incident comes to my mind and will make the point. A large amount was withdrawn from the government treasury. The bill submitted was remarkable. It stated the funds required to build the retaining wall destroyed by recent floods. It also stated an equal amount pending payment for construction of the same wall before the floods, now washed away. The wall was never built because one more flood was expected in a year's time! The money stolen in this way was divided in percentages on a sliding scale to reach ministers at the top and in the case of a bigger haul, the supreme Gaffe sitting in Delhi. A free-for-all in an atmosphere of spurious politics was taken as the norm.

7. Liquid in a container. There are other factors playing a part in the condition of the present economy in Kashmir. The important one is its geopolitical place in the subcontinent. Kashmir, if cut off from its place in the world and pasted in the middle of Europe, would spring into prosperity and rejuvenate its economy instantly, without having recourse to high technology industries. Prosperity would then permeate across borders with help from its tourism and forest wealth alone. Unfortunately, soft borders of a landlocked nation like

Kashmir, surrounded by negative economies, will only have the 'level off' effect; as liquid does in a container.

The area of 86,000 square miles, three times the size of Belgium, the Netherlands and Luxembourg combined, cradling a small number of twelve million people, a meagre 140 people to a square mile could be a recipe for comfort! Kashmir is blessed with talented people and fertile land. The two million Kashmiris in Pakistan and the rest of the world are a major proportion of the labour force indispensable for Kashmir. The trained young people living abroad are an inevitable brain-drain. They would easily be absorbed back into a vacuum.

The people of Kashmir are a proud, self-reliant society. They have kept the wheels of their economy turning over in spite of repeated predacious incursions and regimes bent upon spoils for themselves, leaving the country in an abysmal state.

The hard core of a sustainable economy in Kashmir has two main components. The human factor and natural resources. Both factors have suffered immeasurably. The repressive rule combined with unregulated capitalism, red in tooth and claw, have been stalking Kashmir's economy. A 'nature perfected' garden of the world is a cherished dream. It would have a special niche in the map of the world.

Kashmir is very fertile and abundant in its resources. The soil alone could feed its people with more to spare. The merciless denuding of the forest has reduced the mineral content of the alluvial soil washed down from the unsupported mountains and is full of silt. This soil is normally full of nutrients and fertile. Mountain streams which build the alluvial soil have dried up due to a reduction in the size of glaciers.

Kashmir on the subject of economy can be comparable to other nations of the world.

Like *New Zealand* it is a pastoral land of plenty! Kashmir has 50% more pasture land than New Zealand, the biggest exporter of lamb and its by-products.

Bigger than *Finland*, the mountains of Kashmir lie in the paradise of a boreal coniferous zone. Finland is the second largest exporter of forest products in the world. It has one of the richest Western economies. Even a 10% share of this market would make a lot of difference for Kashmir.

Bigger than *Switzerland* it has the magnificence of natural beauty. Switzerland has more income from tourism than the whole Asian subcontinent together. Kashmir can catch up with the standards of popular holiday resorts and earn a substantial foreign exchange.

Scotland and Kashmir could be paired as twin ecological entities. Cashmere, angora and lambswool are produced in Scotland. Kashmir tweed is comparable to cloth from the Isle of Harris. A place called Paisley in Scotland has been named after a design in shawls imported from Kashmir. The golf courses in Kashmir can be brought up to international standards. There is so much more common ground between the two places, like trout streams, game reserves, lakes and beautiful countryside. Scotland has a constant source of income from exports of wool and woollen products. Why not Kashmir?

Like *Scandinavian countries*, Kashmir has the world's best resources of environmental clean energy. Less than 10% of the resources are exploited.

Like *Iran*, the most exquisite handicrafts comparable to the quality from Iran, are produced in Kashmir. Silk carpets are the pride of Kashmir, unmatched anywhere in the world.

Like *China*, Kashmiri caterpillars weave the finest silk cocoons in the world. Unfortunately all the mulberry trees vanished, and caterpillars with them!

Like *France*, the pure spring waters cascade down the hills, enough to feed a continent. One bottle of French spring water is around 80p. The potential is colossal! The vineyards of Kashmir have been expunged. Grape juice bottled and exported can be a billion-dollar industry.

Like *Austria*, Kashmir has the most magnificent natural slopes for skiing.

The countries used for comparison are rich by virtue of an asset they possess. Kashmir has it all. Each attribute only half exploited must add up to a viable and respectable economy.

The wealth of Kashmir has essential ingredients that need to be elaborated upon. This knowledge is the mainstay of the argument with independence-seeking political parties and the people who follow them. It will also be essential for those people in Kashmiri politics who want accession to India or Pakistan. They can negotiate terms of reference from a position of respectable economical strength and self-reliance, instead of placing a begging bowl on the table. In recent years it has been made known by the pro-Indian lobby that many billions of rupees have been siphoned into Kashmir to maintain its survival. That is a demeaning position for Kashmiris to be in. That kind of relationship is manifestly flawed.

The essential component, the economy, in Kashmir will mainly rest on the following:

1. Agriculture.

2. Horticulture.

3. Water and Power Generation.

4 Livestock and Wildlife.

5. Forest and Forest Products.

6. Trade and Industries.

7. Arts and Crafts.

8. Tourism and Health Farms.

9. Foreign Exchange.

1. *Agriculture*

"The Saffron, iced water and grapes which are rare even in heaven are common here."

Kalhana in *Rajtarangini*.

Agriculture has four essential ingredients which it needs to survive: soil, water, sunshine and manpower.

The Soil

There is potential in the fertile soil of Kashmir to yield enough produce for the populus with plenty more to spare. Alluvium washed down the deltas of mountain rivers and streams is very rich in mineral content. The forests having been mercilessly denuded, has caused soil erosion. Sand and rock is mixed in the silt that comes down. The quality of the soil has degenerated. The soil of Kashmir was unmatched for its fertility. The soil which produced the Saffron crocuses was of a special quality not found elsewhere. The mountain slopes and swamps constitute a big percentage of its soil. Most of this is not arable but with an extra effort the slopes can be terraced like the farms of Southern Italy and cultivated. The swamps are left wild in most places. The growth of willows and grass can be developed in this land. These swamps skirting round the arable land can be drained and restored to full use. The Kerawa soil on the top of plateaux and meadows constitutes the grazing pastures and on it wild flowers with medicinal value grow. The wealth of produce from the Kerawa soil has not been exploited to its potential.

Agriculture in Kashmir is atavistic and possibly, for political reasons, kept that way. The land is fragmented, either drowned in water or scorched. The tilling and harvesting is done manually as in ancient times. The amount of fertiliser used or the type of treatment of the soil required is not controlled. Soil sample surveys, investigations and modern methods of farming are far from realisation.

The floating gardens are a novel method of creating soil in water adopted by Kashmiris over the years. The only snag is, chunks of soil can be poled away and stolen! The soil is made from six feet strips of lake reed or lotus roots, reinforced with mud to form a raft. The land, being buoyant, is anchored to a secure place and used to grow vegetables of all kinds.

Water for irrigation is available everywhere. The distribution and supply will need to be regulated. The high-lying land and kerewas can also be irrigated if the resources are made available.

The valleys of Kashmir have about two hundred days of sunshine. Across the Pir Panjal range the sun is out for more than three hundred days of the year. The problem has always been to protect produce from excess sun, rather than not having enough of it.

Manpower in Kashmir used in agriculture is dedicated and proficient. However, the curse of civilisation has kept the young farmers away from their land. They travel for cheap labour or for a paltry education. The concept of educated farmers and the respect it has in the West is absent. Agriculture as a career is not sought by village boys, even if they own family land.

The crops in Kashmir can be grown in abundance. Rice, wheat barley, mustard and so many other varieties of crops are grown. There is no will, no political motivation and no available energy to employ modern technology in farming. Rice is the staple diet. Maize, wheat, millet, hops, pulses, sesame seeds, barley, poppy, flax, and in hot places cotton, tobacco and sugar cane can be grown.

The vegetables used to be produced even on rooftops or the tops of fencing walls. The recent cheap import of fresh vegetables killed the initiative of the vegetable farmer. There has not been any attempt made to reform the centuries-old methods of obtaining raw sewage from open toilets and using this as manure. The distribution of nitrogen fertilisers has been without control or planning. The genetic engineering and rotational crop growing methods are a far cry away. Modern methods of farming, even using organic fertilisers more suited to Kashmir, have produced abundant crops in some countries. Kashmir has been allowed to slip in the opposite direction and produce less. The grain is distributed on subsidised rates and the market is flooded with imported eggs, chicken, vegetables and even fruit, which Kashmir is so famous for. Local produce of vegetables, like potatoes, greengages, asparagus, tomatoes and all others in common use, were grown in abundance. The sugar beet has not been cultivated in Kashmir. It could be used to extract sugar, at present imported into Kashmir at high cost. Asparagus farmers are exporting the vegetable to hotels in Bombay. The quality has never been upgraded. This is an expensive delicacy and could be valuable to the economy. Maple trees can be cultivated and exploited for sugar, very much in demand.

Tea is grown in Lehjan along the Caspian border of Iran and the Assam hills. The terrain is similar in parts of Kashmir. There may be a possibility of exploring that avenue. Tea is a very lucrative foreign exchange earner.

The fruit industry of Kashmir was flourishing. Kashmir is the veritable garden of fruit in Asia. The indigenous growth of pears, apples, vine, mulberry, cherry, peach, apricot, plum, melon, pomegranate, raspberry, gooseberry, figs, and nuts of all kinds, including walnuts, almonds, hazel nuts, water chestnuts (singhara), and others are abundant. The most exotic and luscious exuberance of tasty fruit gave Kashmir its good name. 'Your face is like an apple from Kashmir', an expression which is used to exalt the beauty of women by their lovers all over the subcontinent. All varieties grown are famous. The Golden Delicious, White Red Spot, Granny Smith, and cooking apples have been grown. One cooking apple called 'Bamczoont' is dried in the sun, preserved and cooked with lamb during the winter. The recipe is so delicious my mouth is watering now as I am writing!

Nuts like pistachios have never been tried to be grown in Kashmir, even though the soil is contiguous, in certain places, with Afghanistan.

Fruit is exported to India in wooden boxes as it was two hundred years ago! A big drain on wood reserves. Recycled materials are used all over the world for this purpose. The fruit related industries are almost non-existent. One or two canning factories sprang up and then whittled away. Fruit and vegetable related industries, if modernised, can sustain a prosperous life for a lot of people in Kashmir, but there is no political will, there is no transport like a railway and there is no electricity!

2. *Horticulture*

Kashmir has been described as a garden of Paradise. One reason is the exquisite array of flowers both cultivated and growing wild. Gulmarg, meaning 'meadow of flowers', was named after its treasure of wild flowers. The roses of Kashmir have been circulated and grown from seeds all over the world. One particular variety is the perfumed Rose of Kashmir. It is not good-looking but the essence is very pleasing. Perfumes and essential oils can be produced and exported to earn substantial foreign exchange. Unfortunately, all the perfumeries are in other countries and Kashmir just provides the flowers. Seed farms have been run successfully but no attempt has been made to modernise the industry. In the paradise of flowers the only garden centres to be seen are flower laden small boats, 'Shikaras'. The potential for growth is tremendous.

There are over five hundred varieties of flowering plants in Kashmir. The notable flowering shrubs are thyme, vine, clover, bramble, heather, ivy, honeysuckle, chrysanthemum, thistle, lilac, Jacob's ladder (Gulmarg), sage, and a lot of others.

The flowers which bring the colour of the season bloom in spring are iris, narcissus, tulips, bluebells, crown imperial, and lilac. Nishat and Shalimar gardens have an array of daffodils, pansies and scented geraniums. The Almond Blossoming is a special occasion for Kashmiris. Picnics in almond orchards were popular. The water chestnut vendors and little girls, making necklaces from petals dropped from the trees, bring a lot of charm to the place. This festival marks the start of the spring and is an exhilarating experience.

The summer flowers like carnations, roses and peonies, fill all the gardens. The flower vendors are out selling to the tourists (in more peaceful times).

The autumn colours from chinar leaves and water lilies and lotus flowers all make Kashmir a special place in the world for its exquisite beauty. Autumn also has the abundance of fruit which is not imported from outside and has a special quality to its texture and taste.

The medicinal plants which can be exploited for substantial revenue are aconite to yield digitalis; poppy is grown for opium products; and violets, mints and daphnia etc., for other medicinal products. The Drug Research Laboratory in Rajbagh Kashmir produced pharmaceutical products and used local plants and herbs. It was closed down.

3. Water and Power Generation

A sound political system is imperative for the preservation of water assets in Kashmir. Kashmir has no oil wells, but simple water, exemplary in quality and unmatched in taste is a precious commodity. Water used in agriculture, the energy sector, transport and drinking water from the famous springs can all add up to a substantial support to the state's coffers. There are two main sources of water in Kashmir.

a. Rain, snow and the glaciers.

b. Ground Water.

a. Rain, Snow and the Glaciers.

The rivers and streams from the Himalayan mountains make Kashmir a resourceful country. The low-lying areas are deluged with abundant water but the upper Kerawas are dry. This waste of cultivable land has not been exploited. The water from the rivers escapes and creates swamps called 'Nambal'; the rest flows into paddy fields or kuhls by means of gradient irrigation.

Surface water produced from rain and melting snow and glaciers is abundant. The run-off escapes into rivers, lakes and swamps. The rivers are gushing with water during the summer months fed by the streams of the great mountain ranges. Water from the Pir Panjal mountains is mostly from the rainfall. The glaciers melt to feed the streams which run in confluence to form the rivers.

The annual rainfall ranges from 579mm in Badgam to 1005mm in Handawara or 1195mm in Doru. There are dry spells and drought in the high-lying areas which are variable. Srinagar experienced nineteen droughts in a cycle of seventy-two years, lasting anything up to six months, on the other hand, floods have inundated crops and created a crisis.

Floods are common in Kashmir. Plenty of water has also meant problems with over-abundance. Sadly, the implications for the farmers are great and grain is washed away and fodder for animals becomes scarce. Corrupt successive governments and their civil engineers have made a fortune out of this adversity. Flood control and remedial measures taken become lucrative for civil officers. Avarice is the spur of administration in Kashmir. Diversionary canals have been ill-conceived and have failed to avert disasters.

The overspill of flood water, however, gets absorbed by low-lying swamp land or Nambals, like Batmalu, Hokarsar, Nougam and others, and lakes like the Wular, Dal, Nagin, Anchar. An estimated 120,000 cusecs of water is absorbed by this depressed basin. The outlet of the Jhelum at the Baramulla gorge is narrow and lets through only about 28,000 cusecs of water every year.

Floods have been made worse. The outlet waterways have been filled instead of creating more. The Nala Mer project is an example. A beautiful waterway was filled and a road built on it. The silt has been allowed to accumulate and settlements were built on river banks. All these factors have made the river smaller and the affluent bigger. The rivers and streams have also been made dirty, teeming with overgrown weed and rife with bacteria from raw sewage. Cholera and shigella epidemics have become common now.

b. *Ground Water*

Kashmir is blessed with plenty of water, therefore no attempt has been made to exploit this source. The dry Kerawas and the thousands of acres of now non-arable land could be cultivated and give Kashmir the proud place of self-sufficiency, if this water was exploited where needed. The only water from this source are the natural springs – the most beautiful water on earth! And plenty of it.

How could Kashmir turn its water resource into gold? Water and agriculture go hand in hand and prosperity follows behind. Modernisation of agriculture and irrigation can turn the fields of Kashmir into a haven for green gold.

Water Used for Transport and Navigation. The network of waterways which existed before the Nala Mer canal, now filled by town planners, made Kashmir the 'Venice of Asia'. The Jhelum is still used for transporting passengers and building materials for long distances. The forest wealth from Kashmir used to be transported through Jhelum into what Pakistan is now and to the rest of the world. Logs felled from the forests are easily transportable by rivers. Passengers are transported, and the service can be run in the same way as Bangkok or Venice.

Water for Drinking and Domestic Use. A bottle of spring water from Scotland or France will cost around eighty pence, equivalent to forty Indian rupees per bottle! Water from some Kashmiri springs can be claimed to be of a superb quality. The potential for turning water into wealth is tremendous. Drinking water supplies in the villages are still from the streams and rivers. There are no taps and piped water supplies.

Rivers of Kashmir

Kashmir, embroiled in the meshes of politics, has been set back still further because India and Pakistan are fighting over water rights from rivers coming out of Kashmir. The Indus Water Treaty was signed by the two countries – Pakistan has a claim on the waters from the Indus, the Jhelum and the Chenab, along with their tributaries. Kashmir has prior rights over its rivers and can claim compensation or a trade agreement to barter for the import of commodities. Kashmir waters irrigate most of Punjab and feed very big dams. It is a wealth from which Jammu and Kashmir must have the major share.

Energy Sources

Hydroelectric Power Generation. The most tenable asset in Kashmir is the environmentally clean, cheap and reliable source of energy from water. Attempts to exploit this great source of energy have been stymied by politicians with vested interests. Many projects were started and subsequently aborted. The World Bank has financed the Lower Jhelum project but political upheavals and corruption hindered progress. The Swedish contractors are working in Uri and the French consortium have taken up the Dolhasti NHPC project in Doda. Industries cannot be established due to the paucity of power and the only electricity people see is a dim light for two hours in the evening; so dim that, people say, you need to find the light with a candle! The cruel irony is that what power there is has been exported to India, hooked onto the national grid.

The existing capacity of power generation is very meagre. Ganderbal power house generates 15,000kWs and Mohra 6,000kWs. Clubbed together, the total supply for all Kashmir is a meagre 21,000kWs. Most of the villages and far-flung areas are still burning resin laden wood for light. Electricity from the Chenani project (Jammu) was supposed to fill in a part of the dire need in Kashmir through a 220kV transmission line. The transmission line has not been installed and Kashmir is still in darkness. The Upper Sindh and Lower Jhelum projects are still lingering on and in spite of foreign companies financed from outside help, the commissioning of these power houses is far-fetched. There are many other projects which could be feasible. The Chinese engineers suggested a scheme for multiple miniature power houses all over the state, exploiting gradients and volume of water from streams and rivers. The total capacity of energy from water alone can be over 100,000kV (100MW), enough to light up the roads and cater for all domestic and industrial needs.

Kashmir in darkness has been bereft of technological advances, particularly so in the energy sector. People wake up in the mornings to the glimmer of daylight and spend only a minimum time in the dark hours of night. There are no nightclubs for them and life comes to a standstill after dark. At the time of writing, for five years everyone in Kashmir has had to return home before it gets dark. There are curfews in force and chances of getting killed are more likely outside than indoors.

Alternative sources of energy can also be exploited:

Forest Based Fuel. This includes logs, forest waste and trimmings, sawdust and charcoal from wood. The fuel can be used to run generators for electricity.

The Coal Mines in Jammu are productive and have been partly exploited. This coal can be made sulphur dioxide free and used to run the power house.

Solar Power, passive and active. The passive methods include simple measures like south-facing windows, glass panels south-facing, or a conservatory with a trombe wall for absorbing heat, making solar efficient houses. The water in the cylinders is heated by the sun and the house heated with the warm water. In the active method, the photo-voltaic cells act as semi-conductors and convert sunlight into electricity. The cells are expensive but could still be installed in far-flung guest houses and telephone booths.

Straw and Waste. The energy from burning straw and household waste can be harnessed. Organic household waste and sewage from a farm will generate enough electricity to pay for the collection of refuse. There is no refuse collection in Kashmir. Waste paper and refuse burnt in incinerators or broken down by anaerobic digestion and decomposed by bacteria will yield methane gas which can be used as a source of energy.

Wind Power. Wind Power can be exploited in the hills of Kashmir as in no other part of the world. The mountain slopes will always oblige with a burst of stormy winds. The turbines running on wind power may be visually intrusive or noisy, a deterrent in the West, but in Kashmir mountains are so numerous and so far away from inhabited places that these problems will not occur.

Logs of Wood could in theory by used to run turbines. Planting trees in great numbers, like poplar and willows every five years will provide enough firewood for the purpose.

Geothermal energy as a potential source of power is substantial if exploited methodically. Kashmir runs across the volcanic zone and there is energy pent up in the substrata of the foothills.

Kashmir and its people will always be frugal consumers. The total expanse of Jammu and Kashmir will use half of what energy is required for Manhattan alone. Kashmir needs clean electricity to run its transport, including cars. One day, Kashmir, it is hoped, will be environmentally the cleanest place on earth. Scooters and diesel trucks will need to be expunged from its transport system.

Kashmir is the only place like Salk Island in Great Britain, which can be turned green and free from pollution, dust, chemical and nuclear waste, and all harmful gases.

4. *Livestock and Wildlife*

The world's richest repositories of animal wealth are in Kashmir.

There are about five hundred species of animals and more than three hundred families of birds, resident and migratory, in Kashmir. The ecological and political changes must have reduced the numbers. There is no chance of a stocktaking exercise during present times.

The special character, natural features and configuration of the mountains, water and land makes Kashmir an ideal home for all kinds of fauna. The wild animals are an asset, only they have been driven into the depths of the high mountains away from their normal habitats by the ubiquitous presence of the military. Carnivores like snow leopards are a feature of the Liddar Valley. The mongoose, wolf, jackal and fox used to be seen all over the foothills. Pine martens, otters, weasels, (white nosed) have now become almost extinct. The black bear is still seen in Lolab Valley and the brown ones near to maize fields.

The prize animal of Kashmir is easily the hangul, a jungle goat (stag) which weighs about two hundred pounds and used to be common in the Pir Panjal range, Gurez, the Sindh Valley and Lolab. This animal has ruthlessly been killed by the army for its meat. They have receded into the depths of Himalayas above the forest line. The hangul sheds its horns in March and grows them back in autumn. This animal has been preserved in some state sanctuaries, eg, Wangat, Khanmu, and Tral.

The ibex in Lolab and the Liddar Valley has also been hunted, especially for its under fleece. This wool has special characteristics. Other animals like the musk deer, marmot and hare are relics of Gulmarg, Pir Panjal.

"There has been wanton destruction of wildlife and its habitat," says Shafi Khan, the wildlife warden. The Wildlife Protection Act of 1978, passed, was an eyewash for visiting European conservationists. Poaching continued unabated and the ruling factions hunted down the animals and birds in Overa, Shikargah, Khiram, Duksum, and all the wetland reserves like Hygam and Hokarsar.

The economic benefits of these animals are enormous. They not only form a challenging attraction for animal loving tourists but also the wool, the horns and skins of animals permitted for trade have a great potential as economic assets.

The Pashmina Goats in the Aksai Chin area of Ladakh, now occupied by China, yield the most exquisite cashmere wool the world has known. One ton of this wool will be worth one million pounds. The Kashmir Kani Shawl industry depended on this under fleece of the goats. This centuries-old shawl industry was the backbone of Kashmir's economy in the last century. Kashmir will need Aksia Chin back, in order to restore the supply of cashmere wool and the industry. This, for the sake of the goat farmers of Aksai Chin and Kashmir.

Kashmiri Lamb. Meat from the lamb reared in the mountains is of exceptional quality unmatched by any other meat in the world. The texture of meat from New Zealand, India or Europe is good but this meat will nowhere match the quality, taste and texture of meat from the mountains of Kashmir. I used to hang the carcass of a whole lamb in an outside unheated room of my hospital in Gurez, Kashmir. A crust of ice deposited on it. Every day one portion was hacked off and cooked. This meat was so tender and tasty, you could eat it raw! The most tasty meat in the world. Was it the grass from the 12,000 feet pastures or the climate? Unfortunately the farmers work in army camps now and the rearing of sheep has waned. In recent years inferior meat has been imported from India. The hill pastures are not available for grazing. The army occupy thousands of acres of grazing land and the Kerewa.

Birds. Kashmir is a haven for the migratory birds. All common types like swallows, crows, quails, pigeons, coots, gulls, cranes and woodcocks are common. The game birds make Kashmir a special place for the hunter. The snow partridge, snow cock, flying duck, goose, and pheasant make it a paradise come true. The birds can form a great mode of livelihood for thousands of people. Pheasants and ducks are still sold in shops when the hunters can get them!

Fish. Kashmir is full of lakes and streams. The rainbow trout streams are abundant. The mirror-carp has been cultivated in the lakes. The older types of Kashmiri fish have become extinct. The fisheries department can modify and increase the production of fish. The export of tinned and frozen fish can yield enough revenue to fill the coffers of a large community. No attempt has ever been successfully made to harness this source of income. Angling in Kashmir is on a par with Scotland and Colorado in the USA. The streams are teeming with trout and the infrastructure does exist for a decent day out angling, thanks to the British liking for the sport. The trout streams are in the hills. The soldiers visit them frequently, throw a hand grenade in the stream and fish surface with their bellies up. One more meal for the army at a small cost.

5. *Forest and Forest Products – 'Cool Exuberance'*

The huge expanse of forests in Kashmir is a proud feature of the paradise. This is a credible asset and will cushion any adverse economic crisis. Timber alone exported to India in 1947 was worth 2.9 million rupees. It increased to 5.5 million in just two years. The amount must have reached epoch-matching proportions.

Finland, a rich Western country of just five million people with only 2% of the total world's forests, had an income of FIM 46 billion (£6.6 billion; IRs 330 billion) in the year 1994. The forests form 80% of the land and the total amount of wood is 1900 million cubic metres! Undivided, Kashmir could claim more forest, an absolute gold mine in terms of assets.

"In the Himalayan belt from Kashmir to Assam once covered with majestic forests, the slopes below 6000 feet have been denuded. In Kashmir a number of famous forests have been obliterated," Mrs Indira Gandhi, prime minister of India stated.

The forest in Kashmir is what oil is to the Arab countries. The curtain of lush green trees in the backdrop of every mountain is like a stage setting for excellence and charm. These trees have already paid for themselves while they just majestically stand there mopping up all the carbon dioxide, sheltering wildlife and giving cool shade. They are the mainstay of the economy in Kashmir.

Trees common in Kashmir are classified in three main categories.

A. *Low Altitude Temperate Forest* (5000-7500 ft). They are the broad leaf trees like poplars, walnuts, elms, conifers and blue cedar.

B. *The Coniferous Zone.* This extends right across Canada, North Japan, China, Central Asia and Finland. The pines are dense and get denser higher up (7500-10000 ft).

C. *The Alpine Zone.* High up, these trees are relatively safe from plunder. They comprise white birch and stunted junipers.

The forest occupies 60% of the total geographical area of Kashmir. The forest can become the backbone of the economy in Kashmir, if properly managed. Nature has put trees covering the mountains for a definite purpose. They are important for the preservation of the total gamut of land resources. Recent years of indiscriminate denuding of forests have caused soil erosion, excessive run-off from the mountains and degradation of the quality of alluvial soil with harmful effects on agriculture.

Conservation

In Finland the forest is mostly owned by the public. Every citizen is involved with conservation and re-planting. They are a free democracy and everyone is patriotic. In order to expect honest allegiance from a Kashmiri, we have to liberate him from the clutches of outside rule and then he has to unlearn the bad habits acquired over generations of servitude. Not far from Badgam I asked some people from the village, why truckloads of young trees were being carted away. They accepted this was simple theft. "In the old days, there was a forest ranger. We used to dread him. Nobody will ask you these days." There is no love lost between the forest and people. Trees belonged to rulers, they think. They vandalise the forest to avenge the rulers. The measures which may need attention when the situation does normalise, in my opinion, are:

1. Strict control of felling and nomadic grazing.

2. Effective measures taken to prevent soil erosion, like raising and supporting soil under the stock forest.

3. Cordon off bald patches with a fence and replant.

4. Plant trees in new areas and where soil erosion has taken place. (In Finland three hundred million tree seedlings are planted every year.)

5. Provide alternative domestic fuel.

There are specific species of trees suitable for different terrains and selective plantation will restore the treasures of the woods in the Himalayan mountains.

(i)   Cedar is the best timber for building work, seasoned and logged.

(ii)   Blue Pine (Kiaru) is also used as timber for house building and burnt for fuel and charcoal. The resin extracted is used as a protective ointment on legs by farmers and can be used to manufacture oil paints.

(iii)   Spruce (Kachil) timber, not as durable, has been used for shingles and planks.

(iv)   Fir trees have been extensively used for building work.

(v)   Yew trees are used for furniture.

(vi)   Alder trees are used for furniture.

(vii)   The elm trees, a feature of Lolab Valley, are used for furniture and farmers' implements.

(viii) Bird cherry is used for spinning wheels.

(ix)   Ash (Hom) trees provide wooden implements and timber for boats and farms.

(x)   Walnut. There are two varieties of walnut trees. The fruit yielding and the barren tree. Wood carving in Kashmir is an art unsurpassed by any other craftsmen of the world. Walnut wood has been exported to Europe in logs and local craftsmen are deprived of the raw material. Walnut furniture of the fruit bearing type has the best grain. The Zangul or barren type has no grain. The trunk has less grain and is brown, while the branches are so light that they need to be dyed with the extract of the shell of the fruit.

(xi)   Poplar. (Phres). The two types, Italian and white, are very common in Kashmir and are used for building and recently for boxes to export fruit.

(xii) Maple. (Kanar). Its golden foliage makes a beautiful contrast to the green surrounding trees. The timber is used for making implements etc.

(xiii) Willow. The weeping willow and erect types are abundant in Kashmir. People still use the twigs for a tooth brush. They just bite the end into a brush. The wood is used for fuel. Willow rushes are used to make a range of furniture, very popular in Kashmir.

(xiv) Birch (Burza) is an excellent fuel. The normal habitat is in the higher mountains. Some trees have still survived.

(xv)   Witch hazel (Poh) has been used with a pestle and mortar for husking rice (Mohul).

(xvi) The chinar is the national tree. The shade from the chinar is extremely cool. Like the poplar they were introduced by the Moguls. Akbar planted over a thousand chinars in Nasim Bagh alone (Hugel). Some chinars were brought down and sold by Mehan Singh, the Sikh governor (Vigne).

(xvii) The spindle tree (Chol). The wood has been used for famous pen boxes and slates for schools.

(xviii) The fruit trees are in abundance and form a big proportion of the economy. The most common are apple, apricot, pomegranate, pear, plum, mulberry, almond, walnut, fig and cherry.

Grasslands. The grazing pastures of Kashmir occupy 10% of the total free area of Kashmir. The alpine grasses in particular are vital for the survival of animal stock and the nomad Gujars who rear them.

Forest Based Industries

The people in Kashmir were not allowed to develop any forest based industry. Applications by industrialists were referred to New Delhi and turned down. The forest can yield raw materials for manufacturing industries. Some items can be discussed.

1. Paper: printing, writing

2. Paper board

3. Recyclable virgin fibre

4. Chipboard

5. Veneering products

6. Timber for construction, railway sleepers

7. Furniture

8. Sporting goods

9. Matchboxes

10. Resin and gloss paints

11. Wood for fuel

12. Forest waste for power generation

Paper mills need large amounts of water and wood. Mills can be established for making pulp and supplied with power from paper producing mills. The residue from the pulp is used to generate power and that in turn runs both types of mill. The water can be put back in reservoirs and recirculated.

Paper is a very precious commodity and always in demand. In 1994 the export value of paper alone from Finland was Finnish Mark (FIM) 46 billion or £6.5 billion. In terms of the Indian currency, that amounts to Rs 325 billion. Finland has 2% of the world's forests and exports 10% of the paper. That kind of money could work wonders for Kashmir, given half a chance!

The Middle Eastern countries are clamouring for paper and paper products, like cartons, plates, cups, bags, and many other consumer items for daily use.

Paper Board is compressed paper mixed with bonding material. This is extensively used in packaging boxes. A factory in Kashmir would thrive.

Recycled Virgin Fibre is a new concept of obtaining paper fibre from waste products. In the paper industry these days nothing is discarded. Water is used again, and energy to drive the plants is retrieved back by running turbines with the waste which in turn fuels the mills.

Chipboard manufacture is a revolution in the building and construction industry. The raw material is only the forest waste and sawdust. Chipboard makes partitions, ceilings, cabinets and furniture, saving timber, a valuable resource. No factory was allowed in Kashmir.

Veneering plants were set up in Kashmir in the Pampore area. The products were good quality. The veneering sheets made a finished surface look like pine, walnut, oak. I covered my lounge walls with remarkable results. The factory is now closed.

Timber for Construction and Railway Sleepers. This forms the main use of trees felled in Kashmir. Logging has denuded forests in Kashmir. Politicians extracted a price from this wealth for propping up a regime. The rich forest contractors were relatives or accomplices of ministers in power.

Furniture making has never been encouraged in Kashmir. Furniture is imported from Punjab, when the raw materials used are exported from Kashmir. Kashmir can become the world's finest walnut, cane and traditional furniture production source. The industry presently is very sketchy and has waned.

Sporting Goods have never been manufactured in Kashmir on a tangible scale. Material for the manufacture of cricket bats, tennis rackets, hockey sticks, or even the toy versions of these items is available and the craftsmen are the best in the world, given a chance!

Match factories were closed in Baramulla and other places. The material to make this product was instead exported to India and Indian matchboxes appeared on the market. This is a very lucrative industry and can employ plenty of labour force.

Resin from the trees is a valuable resource. Licences were issued to political favourites to extract this material from the forests. The few people chosen, made money by ripping the trees apart and exporting the resin to India. No attempt was ever made to manufacture gloss paints or other products from this raw material.

Wood has been almost the only source of fuel for people to heat and cook with. The corrupt politicians and forest officers made money by allocating big chunks of forest for this use. The gas bottles imported into Kashmir are so scanty that it only provides a meagre 1.5% of the fuel requirement of the state. Any future alliance of Kashmir with India or Pakistan has to put gas and petrol requirements as priority on the list. Gas supplied to households will save the sacrilege of forest denudation.

Forest chippings and waste can also be used to run electricity generation turbines. The one message which stands out is to plant trees and plant more trees. Most comforts of life can be derived from this resource.

6. *Trade And Industries*

"The Kashmir Valley is to a great extent a self-supporting country." (Walter Lawrence, *The Valley of Kashmir.*)

Given a mode of transport and routes to travel, Kashmir would always be on a positive balance of exports. The finished products from plants, drugs and chemicals, flora and fauna, fibres like wool and silk, forest products, fruits and oil seeds and oil, hides and skins made into finished products and famous handicrafts exported would offset the imports of salt, sugar, tea, tobacco and petroleum products. The export of agricultural products can reach astronomical proportions. The industry requires a thorough reshuffle and the introduction of modern methods of cultivation, and exploration of the manufacture of native raw materials within Kashmir.

Industries

The rest of the world is making tremendous strides. The name, "Industry", became an easy tool to extract profits from raw materials and subsidies. The subsidies were given on political grounds. Land was allocated for some units. That land is still left abandoned and the derelict sheds tell the story of the deceit in the industry of Kashmir.

The industries which can thrive, utilising local talent, local raw materials, local geography and climate go into the hundreds, but the main industry must be the paper, textiles, leather, precision high technological industries, and a multitude of others.

7. Arts and Crafts

By far the most credible and everlasting asset of Kashmir is her people. Their inherent ability to create wealth with their hands has been known for centuries.

Hands of Gold

The industrial sphere has always been based exclusively on their art work and diligence. The outstanding items are shawls of all grades from Jamawars (pure cashmere with needle work all over), circulating in very exclusive elite circles of Paris, to run-of-the-mill widely used woollen shawls in Bengal.

Cashmere shawls were held in great esteem all over Europe. The ring shawl, two and a half yards long, could be threaded through a small ring! It is soft to touch but very warm and a great comfort to feel.

Josephine Bonaparte was the proud owner of a large selection of Kashmiri shawls. Paris was the fashion centre of the world and the shawls were amongst the most revered. The woollen tweeds and materials, blankets and jumpers are hand knitted from home spun yarn. Cashmere wool itself came from the specially bred goats from Ladakh and the Aksai Chin areas of the state. Unfortunately, China has occupied that part of the country, and this valuable material is scarcely available.

Kashmiris have turned everything they touched into gold. They have a good pair of hands in creating designs original to Kashmir. These designs were then copied in Europe, especially Scotland, notably the tear drop or 'paisley'. People in Scotland were taught these designs and they started making shawls.

The other items produced and which stand out as Kashmiri are embroidery sets, crewel curtain material and chain stitch rugs. Woodwork includes excellent walnut wood carving, and extremely adroit carpentry and furniture making. The ceilings made from wooden tiles held together as diamonds with tongue and groove joints are very special. Willow baskets and furniture have much potential for Kashmir. Homespun wool and cloth made into blankets and jackets have been indispensable for local use in harsh winters. Papier maché articles made from pulp and beautiful lacquered patterns by the Naqash artists of Kashmir are outstanding. These boxes and bowls and Easter eggs can be seen in shops all over the world. The other trade in which Kashmir made a mark is pottery. The golden hands of the Kashmiri potters can only be appreciated if you visit these shops. They even created their own designs for pipes and plumbing traps.

Copper work, making utensils and Samawars, was a flourishing industry at one time. The silversmiths of Kashmir have produced a galaxy of very exuberant silverware and many homes round the world are proud to own silver from Kashmir. Silver came via Yarkand into Kashmir or else rupee silver was melted and used.

Jewellery. The Gada Bazaar was famous in the fourth bridge area of the capital city for the creation and fashioning of the most fantastic semi-precious stones in the world. The engravers excel in turquoise and enamel in silver. There has been very little interest in mining and geological surveys. In 1882 in the Pedar Valley, Sapphire was discovered. In Kishtawar and Doda semi-precious and precious stones have been detected.

Leather made from goat skins is plentiful. The hide from cows is not available. Cow slaughter is illegal in Kashmir, but the hide is freely imported from India (cows are sacred in India but the hide is still available). Leather was tanned and processed locally and made into many utility items from handbags to shoes and jackets etc. Embroidered leather was in great demand.

Gunsmiths and surgical instrument makers were very popular. Operations were performed in hospitals with instruments made locally! The handmade guns were of a high quality.

The handicraft artists of Kashmir passed these crafts down the generations within their families. This group of people have suffered even with the talent and diligence they have. They were poor and exploited. It is amazing how a few have survived. Godfrey Vigne, the French traveller, relates an experience. He asked a well-known wood carver to make him a model of a mosque. He deliberately made mistakes in the carving. Vigne, not pleased, asked the reason for the shoddy workmanship. In confidence he replied, "I make mistakes on purpose, so the Sikh governor does not get to know my good work. He would make me a slave and take all I earn." The Sikh soldiers frequently accosted him and took his money.

Francois Bernier in 1663 remarked that Kashmiri art will die off because, "Indians regard not the beauty and excellence but the cheapness of the article." That was a prediction made three centuries ago. Even today there is truth in it.

The facade of the Delhi Coronation Durbar in 1911 for King George V was made with the wood carvings and decorations of papier maché of Kashmiri craftsmen. They were highly appreciated and considered as the pinnacle of craftsmanship by the King.

In the Second Sikh War, the British captured Toshkhana in Lahore from Ranjit Singh. Inside they found the golden chair of Ranjit Singh, the Kohinoor jewel and rooms full of Kashmiri shawls wrapped in bales. They were a part of his acquisitions taken by force from shawl makers.

Carpet Industry

The carpets of Kashmir are sold in every part of the Western world. The revolution in Iran was a chance for the Kashmiri carpets to get a boost. Handmade, hand knotted carpets are made from silk, wool, wool and silk in combination. The yarns can be mixed in the weaving process. The yarn laid across lengthways on the loom (warp) can be woven into by filling yarn interlacing (weft) to the finished edges (selvage) in any combination, eg all silk, all wool, all cotton or silk and wool etc. The other material used is staple or mercerised cotton. It takes six months' weaving for one man to produce a nine foot by six foot carpet, depending on how close knit the carpet is woven; 18/18 knots per square inch or 22/22, per square inch. The silk carpet from Kashmir is the best buy in the world. The craftsmen in Kashmir have made carpets of exceptional quality with an unmatched record of 90 knots per square inch.

Handicrafts in Kashmir need a revival. Cheap merchandise production will need to be discouraged and quality controlled. The potential for growth is colossal.

8. *Tourism and Health Farms*

Kashmir has always been prized for its natural attributes, qualities and resources for tourism. The political situation in Kashmir has never been tranquil enough to develop its potential for first class tourism.

An attempt was made in 1909 to establish the 'Motamid Durbar', a kind of tourist office. The Maharaja was strict on tourists. Even the British had to register, and only occupied houses in Munshi Bagh and Sheikh Bagh. The Nedus Hotel was opened in 1900. Every week, the 'Peston Ji Auctions' in front of his 'white horse' were held and all British imported items left by departing servicemen were bought by eager customers.

The measly 3,700 tourists who visited Kashmir in 1949 had only 426 from Europe and the USA. A better record was set in 1954 at 21,000. In 1982 a record number of 600,000 tourists entered Kashmir, of which 50,000 were from a different continent. The numbers dwindled rapidly afterwards. These figures are so paltry for a place with the magnificence of Kashmir that it is not a fraction of the numbers visiting the Algarve coast in Portugal alone! Until recently an influx of people escaping the heat of the Indian places inundated the streets of Kashmir. The abundance has been overwhelming and food supplies were depleted. The attics of city houses normally inhabited by the house cats were converted to accommodate the deluge of visiting people. Many thousands of professional beggars also hitchhiked from India and descended upon the cities, in order to get away from the seething summer heat and get some money begging on the streets. The influx is impossible to control with open borders.

Kashmir offers every kind of attraction for Western tourists. There is sport, varied and excellent, scenery for the artist and layman, mountains for the climber, flowers for the botanist, vast fields for the geologist and magnificent ruins for the archaeologist. The Epicurean will find plenty of fruit and vegetables and the lounger has houseboats under chinar trees. The varying climate, the water and the change of air will restore an invalid. "A day will come when Kashmir will become the health resort of the world." (Walter Lawrence, *The Valley of Kashmir*).

Kashmir has the potential of providing a health inspiring, invigorating and entertaining holiday for at least five million visitors a year. The facilities provided for all those who come will have to match other resorts of the world. Even the Arab, and high profile religious cities like Dubai have started beach tourism! There is everything in Kashmir that nature can provide. It needs what man can do to complement its resources. It is essential not to lose sight of the tourist from the Asian subcontinent. Western tourists usually prefer holidays full of sun, sand, water, wine and idle lounging. That still leaves a hard core of tourists from all over the world who would only choose to come to Kashmir for tranquillity and recuperation. The standards have to be raised, and selected tourists coming through reputed travel agencies encouraged.

It seems pointless to elaborate on all the tourist attractions Kashmir offers as they are common knowledge, albeit it is expedient to make a reference to the unusual features in the itinerary of a delightful holiday.

Gulmarg. The golf course in this 'Flower Meadow' was laid out by Sir Neville Chamberlain (field marshall in the British army in India). At one time there were three courses here, two eighteen-hole and one nine-hole. In the hot season, Gulmarg had a population of 10,000, mainly Europeans housed in cottages scattered and hidden behind the pine trees. No Indians were allowed. At 8,500 ft, this is the highest golf course in the world. In the middle of the basin was an exquisite shopping centre made into a circle and beautiful shops sold everything from furs and jewellery to golf bags and equipment. The total complex was bulldozed and flattened. The idea was to enhance the views of Gulmarg, conceived by a ruler with little experience or background. Living in Gulmarg was a phenomenon impossible to emulate in any other part of the world. There was no dust, no cars, or trucks. Horses were the only mode of transport available, a wonderful experience! Gulmarg has changed now but the saving grace is that it can be restored back to its glory.

The houseboats are a special attraction in Kashmir. They are colourful and very well maintained. The only problem that needs to be resolved is the drainage of sewage and effluents. The British were not allowed to buy land. In 1880, the Englishman, M.T. Kennard solved the problem by designing a houseboat for himself. The idea caught on and there are many thousands of houseboats moored along the rivers and lakes of Kashmir, emulating British traditional style, steep gables, shingled roofs, Tudor-style timbering, interior decor and a rose garden outside the moorings. All the English names are displayed in rows.

The ancient treasures have been mercilessly vandalised by the incumbent rulers and ignorant members of the public.

Inside the Shalimar garden during Shah Jehan's time the black marble pavilion was gilded with Persian inscriptions saying, 'If there is paradise on earth it is here, it is here.'

The grey stone mosque built by the Mogul prince Dara Shikoh near Fort Hari Parbat, and the town built by Akbar, at the gateway to Nagar are reduced to ruins. The Pather Masjid, an all stone mosque built by Nur Jehan, still stands, thanks to political rallies and its constant use for prayers.

9. Foreign Exchange

An estimated two billion dollars worth of foreign exchange money is expected per annum from a modest number of half a million tourists spending an average of $400 on a trip to Kashmir. This is a figure which can only be improved upon with better facilities and stable political conditions.

a. Trade and Export

The Indian presidents' award for the best export performance in handicrafts was given to the Indo-Kashmir Carpet Factory. Kashmir carpets and other handicrafts are the prize items of export from Kashmir. The last good year for exports from Kashmir was estimated at $1.5 billion. This performance can only be better during normal conditions. The only finished product exported from Kashmir are handicrafts. There is no manufacturing industry functioning to produce exportable products. A variety of items can be derived from agricultural products, the forest based industry and finished products, like canned fruit or juices, soups of all kinds, spring water, leather wear, silk and woollen materials, watches and electronics. All these could then be exported.

b Manpower Export

This method of earning foreign exchange is one which Kashmir can ill afford. Albeit there are thousands of skilled Kashmiri workers in the Middle East, Europe, the USA, the Far East and Australasia who send money back home to Kashmir at an estimated level of two and a half billion dollars a year, mostly through Pakistan into Azad Kashmir.

Role of the World Bank

The Bank has provided assistance to Kashmir as part of an aid program meant for India and Pakistan as a whole. The International Bank of Reconstruction and Development and its soft loan affiliate, the International Development Association (IDA) have never been directly involved in any projects. The bureaucracy in Kashmir would filter and modify the loan in the manner suitable to them. World Bank officials go round the world and inspect areas where loans and aid have been expended. I witnessed one of these visits. The delegation was met with warm hospitality. High level officials were assigned the job of taking them round to projects assisted by the bank. The most outstanding of all was the restoration of denuded forests. The party were shown little nurseries which the farmers had planted themselves. The billions of rupees meant for reforestation paid by the bank, had only some flimsy private nurseries to show for their efforts. The bank officials were overwhelmed by the hospitality and like any civilised people expected a government to present an honest picture. They were taken for a ride!

India has made repeated broadcasts of its purported aid to Kashmir. The benefits of this "aid" will have to be assessed. Mr Nehru was told about the pillage of Indian money, by his avaricious Chief Minister, Bakhshi. A wise man, Nehru replied, "Only what goes into his stomach is lost," a move for political expediency Nehru was known for.

India is spending a fortune to keep Kashmir. The last nuclear bomb exploded by India cost $1.5 billion. The recent expenditure on Prithvi missile research cost an astronomical sum. This expense for India is related to Kashmir. Mr Dev Nathan, a prominent Indian economist, warned his government that 'India cannot afford conflicts'.

Banking and Finance

Jammu and Kashmir have been a part of the rest of the subcontinent's policy and rupees have been the standard unit of currency. The people of Kashmir working in finance outside Kashmir have a special interest in the subject. KACU (Kashmir Currency Unit) represented as Kc and Diacu (Decimal Currency Unit) Dc are some of the ideas for the future currency in Kashmir. The Kc could for instance be valued at ten Indian rupees and nine Pakistani rupees. The currency can be tied to an outside banking system in India or Pakistan. The foreign currency and loans from the World Bank, UN and other benefactors, like the Middle East and Kashmir-friendly individuals could come straight into the Kashmiri banks. Kashmiri society will be far from being the prolific consumers in the subcontinent. They use the lowest amount of energy and food and can live on very few resources. It may be hand to mouth living but the fiscal profile of Kashmir is commensurate with the self-reliance of a proud society.

10. Education

The people of Kashmir have special needs in education, health and social services. These may not apply or be practised elsewhere in the subcontinent. In education their need is to acquire a special knowledge of ambience in the natural environment. Children will need to learn the cultural background and the essence of their heritage. Kashmiri as a language will need to be enhanced and put back on the social scene. Recent years have seen a remarkable erosion of even the spoken words of Kashmiri or Dogri. The whole curriculum will require a review. Education will thrive with absolute authority resting with an elected local government, involving the people at every stage.

The depth of cultural background and influx of civilisations from different parts of the world makes the people of Kashmir a distinct category. The elocution of local dialects cannot be replicated by people born outside Kashmir. We know of some families from Punjab who settled in Kashmir over fifty years ago. They speak Kashmiri but the local blend is not there.

Education, therefore, has to be tailored to the special needs of the various parts of Kashmir. The people need self-rule and their own elected governments to implement their curriculum, and not follow a curriculum from outside.

Muslims in Kashmir have not been allowed into schools up until Pratap Singh was ruling. They were not allowed in government jobs, if they did get education. They could not join the state army. They were treated as serfs in the society, given the job of cultivating farms and paddy fields in order to pay taxes or work as 'beggar' (forced labour). A minority of Hindu pandits were given the privilege of education in the few schools available. It was common for people to look for a pandit in the village and ask him to read a letter or a notice from the courts. The first time that people were made to realise that education was essential was after the Glancy Commission and through the efforts of the British resident in Kashmir, installed in Partap Singh's time. British tourists introduced spoken words of English. Many Muslims in tourist trades could not read their native language, but they spoke good English! The British missionaries and teachers started schools and instilled the spirit of education.

Future Economy of Kashmir.

This is dependent upon many factors:

(a) Resolution of political strife. The public sector has come to an absolute standstill. There is no activity in the private sector. The net result is devastating for the economy.

(b) Nature of future status. Kashmir as a vassal state of a dominion will progress in the manner in which the central government wants within the budget they provide for development. The people who make the decisions have a perspective of a nation with many other responsibilities in mind and changes will only be supported if they are beneficial to the country as a whole. An example of this development is the drastic changes made in Gulmarg and Pahalgam to accommodate the influx of Indian tourists. Both places have changed beyond recognition! Thousands of cheap cafes and hotels have sprung up, bringing environmental problems like overcrowding, flies and dirty streets.

(c) The aftermath of the revolution. The last five years have seen devastation and all doors to industry were shut. The infrastructure supporting development has been destroyed. The skills have vanished from the scene, the raw materials so vital for industry are depleted and the natural products grown and nurtured for 'Kashmir-specific industry' have suffered tremendously. It is estimated that it will take at least fifty years to bring back all these factors. It is more vital to Kashmir than it has been to Afghanistan to keep a unified polity which will support tourism and all the essential ingredients of that industry. All faiths will have to be tolerant of each other. Arab Muslim countries like Dubai and Bahrain have opened sea beaches for sunbathing tourists for extra income! Kashmir has a lot more to offer to world tourism. It cannot survive as a Tibetan monastery with 'lots of prayers and plenty of sighs'. Kashmir has always been at the forefront of world history and it should maintain that status.

(d) Action must be taken to modernise agriculture. The potential for growth is enormous. A green revolution will bring a harvest of the sweetest potatoes ever grown, the unmatched quality of asparagus and fruits, grape production will explode and saffron will have a luscious crop. Lamb and other animals reared on mountains and Kerewas will make a name for the most delectable and unique quality for export. The facilities for freezing and storage will need to be put in place.

The mainstay of any development in Kashmir is available electricity. Most important of all is to complete the hydroelectric projects quickly and get electricity to be used for fuel, transport and industry.

The supply side of the economy is essential. Kashmir needs to train its work force and attract all skilled young people from all over the world. Kashmiri talent has made a good name in all fields of technology all over the world. This talent is looking for an open door in Kashmir.

NATURE AND ENVIRONMENT

Shangri-La of the East

"Beauty provoketh thieves sooner than gold."

(Shakespeare, *As You Like It*)

It is human nature for some people to go into a garden and pluck a flower and not be content just to behold and appreciate its beauty and aroma. The minions holding political power in Kashmir have over the years been avaricious and through sheer ignorance, despoiled ruthlessly national assets like the forest. The Mogul kings such as Nur-ud-Din Jahangir ruled Kashmir but at least he appreciated its virtues. He left Kashmir more beautiful than he had found it. The British made their mark, even though they were ruling over the head of the Maharaja from a distance. Most of the tourist attractions seen today are a result of the efforts the British hierarchy, made possible by them. The aim of the developments made was less a benevolent gesture by the British and more because they wanted various comforts for themselves during their summer breaks from India. The disciplines of a regulated better educated society, trained to look after the environment and with care for everyday life were enforced by the British. Golf courses with signs like "Indians and dogs not allowed" and penalties for people throwing litter on the road became law. The British in Kashmir had a good time! The Maharaja ruled like a despot but it was the British who had the cream.

'Meem Sahib salam, pat pat gulam' – children on the streets sang those tunes when they saw an English woman walking – 'Madam, greetings to you, we slaves will follow you,' were the words of the verse.

Kashmir with its good looks made a mark in the world. The natural beauty has been described in terms of the 'emerald pastures', 'sapphire water' or 'pearly snow'. The hills have been compared with Switzerland, the lakes with the Bay of Naples, or the Austrian Tyrol and the Lake District of England, all of which would fill the mind of Wordsworth or capture the imagination of Constable. In Kashmir, every hundred feet of altitude brings a new phase of climate and vegetation. The floor of the Valley is flat with a lush patchwork of different shades of green, glinting with waterways that mirror poplars and weeping willows.

The political ferment in Kashmir has been detrimental to the advancement of a clean environment. People from all over the world have always cherished the salubrious attributes of this veritable paradise, and in order to maintain and enhance its virtues, good government is essential.

Biodiversity invokes an ecological interaction between all living organisms from unicellular plants to mammals. This balance of 'living together' has been disturbed in Kashmir. Birds cannot find the insects they eat, insects cannot find the trees they live on, and soil erosion has swept off the earth for the trees to grow in and so on. The equilibrium has suffered due to the altered habitat of the total environment.

The effect of the changes in climate, pollution, denuded forests, and the constant barrage of visiting tourists have caused this ecological disaster. There is an overgrowth of algae in the lakes, and infestations in the trees and crops. The carbon cycle has been broken, because the total CO_2 absorption surface of the leaves is reduced drastically due to a scarcity of trees and the end product of the trees does not get sequestrated back into the soil. The trees are taken away to far off places and disposed of. Wood, coal or even ashes are not received back by the earth. The carbon and mineral contents of the soil are thus depleted.

The climate of Kashmir has changed. Even in Srinagar, only five thousand feet above sea level, every house used to be decorated with a display of icicles from roof verges and outside bathrooms. This has become a rare sight now with global warming making its impact pronounced in Kashmir. Carbon dioxide, with fewer trees to mop it up, accumulates in the atmosphere and causes the greenhouse effect. The atmospheric temperature is raised, which in turn has reduced the size of glaciers. The summertime sunshine was relaxing and free from mosquitoes. The conditions of poor hygiene and sanitation, the horrendous neglect of drainage of human and animal waste, antiquated sewers and puddles of stagnant water everywhere, have converted Kashmir into a cesspool of breeding insects, micro-organisms, flies and vicious mosquitoes.

The desecration of the environment has been systematically accelerated, as if by design, during the last half century. A nonchalant attitude towards the environment was practised soon after the demise of the Maharaja. Penalties imposed by him for felling trees, Mulberry, Chinar or Walnut, were vitiated in order to keep political gangs pleased. The vicious circle of abuse, exploitation and ignorance was taking its toll on plant and animal life.

CFC gases and SO_2 produced in excessive amounts, were making defects in the ozone layer, which in turn let ultraviolet rays through unfiltered. The fast growth of industries in the Indian states bordering Kashmir, manufacturing refrigerators and air conditioners, caused CFC emissions at an alarming rate. This was in violation of the Montreal Protocol of 1987 signed by India. The UV rays cause skin cancers and growth of insects and pests not found normally. The rays also cause the ambient temperature to rise, resulting in the melting down further of the size of glaciers. There is not enough body in the glaciers to produce the streams like Ferozpore Nala in Tangamarg, which we have been used to seeing in the past. The damage is more visible in Kashmir as reported by the cosmic observatories stationed there.

The global CO_2 output per year is 6.7 billion tons. Kashmir has more than its share. The gases are wafted from the Indian subcontinent and the mountains of Kashmir get the brunt and become the veritable poison keg of Asia.

The essential constituents of the environment which are cause for concern are air, water, sunshine, earth and the carbon cycle, trees and vegetation, flora and fauna, mountains, and ecosystem. All these will need to be looked at.

Breathing in the fresh morning air was the most exhilarating experience of a lifetime for anyone visiting Kashmir. The effects of the cool and crisp breeze were stimulating to the mind and spirit alike. In the past, places like Gulmarg were out of bounds for any vehicular traffic. Dust, diesel fumes and noxious gases have now reached even the roof of the world. Military trucks and jeeps roam like monsters through the flowery meadows and green pastures of the hills. Air in Kashmir gets gases like CO_2 and SO_2, unburnt particles of carbon and CFC gases from the whole subcontinent and chemicals from burning oil wells from as far away as Kuwait. The ozone depletion opens a direct corridor for the ultra violet rays and damages life in the forest and its habitat. Horseback transport has now been replaced by thousands of cheap cars and scooters bellowing out clouds of fumes all over Jammu and Kashmir. The plant and animal life have been adversely affected. There has been less snow, smaller glaciers and thinner ice. The overflowing streams have been reduced to a roadside drain! The effects on the supply of water for agricultural irrigation, power generation and alluvial soil available for agriculture have been significantly reduced. The Karakoram and the Pamirs, the roof of the world, form a canopy over the valleys to protect them from polluting gases generated in central Asia. These mountains almost kissing the skies, capped by the magnificence of the glaciers, take the brunt of the poisons wafting in from the plains. The chimneys may not be bellowing out gases in Kashmir but there is plenty in supply from the subcontinent.

Kashmir was a basin of retreat, a mother's lap for comfort, an exquisite spa for health and vitality, a constant source of spiritual inspiration! The ambience of utopia and an ethereal aroma of fresh ubiquitous flowers touched everything.

Mountain tops had an abundance of wild flowers, heather and green grass. Army traffic and heat have wilted away the flowers, taking with them the fragrance in the air. The 'wandering mind syndrome' is my name for a phenomenon experienced by mountain climbers on the peaks and is attributed to the essence emanating from the wild flowers. I think over-production of red blood cells and less oxygen is also a cause. I witnessed an episode during my own travels. We were climbing to the top plateau of 12,000 ft Razdani, one winter's afternoon. Two in the party were uttering confused words.

Our local guide, who was also the postman, slapped one of them hard in his face. "I am sorry I had to slap you on the face," he explained, "otherwise you would have been drifted away by the spirits of the mountain." It surely woke up the bewildered man! "We lose some men every year in these mountains and never find their bodies," the guide was telling us as we continued our journey. Nevertheless, the feeling of a sky of snow beneath us and steep daunting precipices were exhilarating and an eerie experience was under your skin about the spirits and the vanishing people. At times you are very close to nature, as if you had the presence of God Almighty within your breath, not far away from you. It was also great fun, making a hammock from the blanket (chadur) and sledging down a fall of three hundred metres. I saw otters scuttling in the stream at the bottom of the mountain.

The wildlife population has been reduced in all areas of the state and the migrating birds have become extinct in Kashmir. It is a far cry away for nature loving people to see the stupendous wildlife of Kashmir again! The few species nurtured in sanctuaries have survived through special efforts of local game wardens and the fancy of the ruling gentry who liked going hunting for sport. The snow leopard, brown bear and Kashmir's national animal, the hangul, the jungle goats and many other exotic animals have been pushed into the depths of the hostile territory of the Himalayas and Korakoram by military exercises.

Kashmir in the old days was environmentally clean, more by chance than by design. No fossil fuel powerhouses, no refrigerators to speak of, no steam trains and no fumes from vehicular pollution were evident. There was no nuclear waste, and no chemical waste products dumped because there were no industries in Kashmir. The recent changes have produced filth and pollution. The shanty town culture has been introduced. Dirty cafeterias, fuming diesel oil, traffic and sewage overflowing through the streets even in places like Gulmarg, has become a menace for tourism. Kashmir can be an asset for visitors only if it remains clean like a spa town or a basin of retreat.

In recent years there seemed to be a 'free for all' mood in Kashmir. The monstrous buildings and unplanned constructions were allowed to mushroom up despoiling the skyline. The mess has caused a visage incongruous with the aesthetics of the place.

In the world of today smart money spent on environment by the OECD (Organization for Economic Co-operation and Development), is estimated to be $200 billion a year. The global market for environmental energy will grow to a staggering figure of $300 billion by the year 2000. There is no other country in the entire world where the environment can be exploited better than in Kashmir. The vast range of mountains, mighty glaciers, and abundant resources of nature like the wind, rivers, geothermal potentials or solar energy make it the environmental paradise. Kashmir is getting a fraction of its share of the OECD programs. The funds available with the OECD are not only meant to be spent on providing clean energy and saving the earth from the greenhouse effect, acid rain and ozone holes, but also on cleaning the existing industries which are polluting the world's atmosphere. In Kashmir there is immediate need to effect measures to combat pollution. Kashmir and pollution do not blend! People come to Kashmir for the revival of spirits and recuperation. It is supposed to be a composite spa.

Colossal work needs to be undertaken to clean up the mess in Kashmir. Different ways to tackle the problem have been proposed. Maybe one day the place will receive the attention and help it deserves.

(i) *Waste Management.* There are no sewers, dustbins, incinerators or enough treatment plants in Kashmir. There is no large scale recycling project in hand. Household trash, industrial refuse, or agricultural waste is neither cleared efficiently nor recycled. If remedial measures were implemented now, some modern methods of disposal and recycling could be used, which are not only economical but even self-funding. The recycling process can produce fuel and even fibre for use in textiles and paper.

(ii) *Air Pollution Control.* Everyday more noxious gases enter the lush green valleys of Kashmir. Cars, trucks and scooters in the thousands keep streaming in. The fumes, dust and even appliances like refrigerators, previously unknown to Kashmir, (and not necessary) or hairsprays keep rolling in

and emitting chemicals and gases. The transport system has
to be revolutionised. Electricity must, in the end, run
transport and industry. Electricity itself could be produced
from water, wind, the sun and geothermal sources.

(iii) *Water and Effluent Treatment.* Spring water is clean and is
abundant in Kashmir. The treatment plants for treating the
rain and river waters are decadent. The effluent seeps
through the substrata of the soil and even the lakes are being
killed off. Lake Dal has turned red with fungi, growing due
to human effluent making its way directly into the lake water.
Raw sewage is seen welling out of toilet holes from houses
into the streets of the cities, and the lakes from the
houseboats. The sight is simply despicable. Everyone must
have access to a flush toilet. Sewers and soil pipes have to be
installed, otherwise people of the world may call it a 'dirty
paradise!' Modern treatment plants are efficient and recycle
water and vital by-products.

(iv) *Training of Engineers* in environmental skills. These skills are
special and have advanced over recent years. The OECD
funds available for training are not used in Kashmir. Political
will and acumen have to be cultivated to demand these
privileges. The training must be imparted by Western
countries. The techniques in the field have developed very
quickly in recent years and only modern science has answers
for the problems of a poor country.

(v) *Green Markets.* The trend in marketing green products has
taken off like wildfire in the West. Kashmir grew every
vegetable and grain with natural fertilisers. The only
progress Kashmir has seen is an introduction of some
chemicals and preservatives for agricultural and domestic use.
A 'green Kashmir' revolution will conform with organic
farming and pest control without using too many chemicals.

(vi) *Energy Sources and Management.* There is a potential for the
generation of electricity in Kashmir from environmentally
clean sources. The electricity available at present is not
sufficient for use by the majority of people. The alternative

sources of energy are harmful, eg kerosene oil, candles, mustard oil lamps and wood resins.

(vii) All roads require tarmac and all exposed verges have to be covered with grass. Dust can be eliminated.

(viii) Millions of trees need to be planted in every possible place. The mammoth effort has to come from people privately and also the state. The World Bank pays cash for reforestation. In time, the trees will contribute enormously towards the betterment of the environment.

The mountains. The stupendous magnificence of the Himalayas and Karakoram stand so proudly over the valleys that people feel as if Mother Nature is holding them in her arms. To the north there is a veritable promontory of Nanga Parbat (26,620 feet above sea level); to the east is Haramukh (16,903 feet). In the south is the Mahadev Range (up to 17,800 feet) and Amarnath (17,320 feet). Flying over to Kashmir from India along the south-eastern borders, will bring into view the snow-capped mountains of the Pir Panjal Range (up to 15,000 feet) Further north of Kashmir the precipice of Tosh Maidan (14,000 feet) and the snow-capped Kazi Nag stand majestically.

The mountains are carpeted with firs and pines. Mountain streams come tumbling down through the trees with cold, crisp, and clean water. The banks of the streams are adorned with a luscious growth of flowers. The clematis, honeysuckle, jasmine and wild roses emit the ineffably exhilarating fragrance.

Gulmarg is an 8000 foot high valley named after the fragrant wild flowers which embellish the plateaux. One night's stay in the 'Hansel and Gretel' type wooden huts overlooking the magnificent expanse of the golf course and the snow clad peaks of Khilan Marg, will be a once in a lifetime experience. You wake up to be greeted by the cool and fresh morning air which penetrates your soul. You instinctively breath in long breaths and with wide open eyes behold the scenery!

The forest supplies the fuel, timber and other forest products so vital for the economy of Kashmir. The mountains provide vast areas for the grazing of animals. The best of the grazing is higher up where the firs and pine in the forest are replaced by the birch. The denuded mountains need to be covered with trees.

The Lakes. The popular legend is that Kashmir was once a huge lake! The water found a cranny in the mountains at a pass near Uri Baramulla and drained away the lake, surfacing land. The original inhabitants of Kashmir lived on the water. This Reverine civilisation of people persists even today. They live in boats all year round. Water remained the hallmark of transport. Waterways, lakes and rivers formed a network from one mountain range to another. Doongas (living-in boats) comprise two or three rooms roofed over by shingle and moored along rivers and lakes.

The lakes have shrunk recently due to neglect. The glaciers and streams have been reduced in size. The Wular, Mansbal and Dal lakes are outstanding. They freeze over during the harsh winters making it possible to walk and cycle across the ice. All the lakes are in urgent need of deweeding and dredging, otherwise they will die!

The glaciers tucked away in the northern mountains melt and create the rivers which traverse through Kashmir and irrigate the vital expanse of the subcontinent.

The environment of Kashmir has changed. Political motivation, an indomitable resolve and a lot of hard work is essential to restore the glory of this forsaken Shangri-La.

THE FUTURE OF KASHMIR

The Dawn Mist

They hear voices telling them what to do. The voices come from God!

By and large, the people of Kashmir from the core of their hearts want a home free from outside control and their own suffrage, governing their destiny. Their relations with the subcontinent are insuperable but they are looking for a niche in the map of the world. Any form of political system which keeps the so-called 'Kashmiriat' within its curtelage has a chance to succeed. As a society people believe in composite nationalism and a *laissez faire* policy towards their neighbours. The first call for all politicians is to underpin confidence in people and give them their identity.

Fly thee my beautiful rose
Tell them all, friends and foes

                    Home it is, our life and soul
                    Free Kashmir our only goal

Our object is our country
nothing but our country

                    We will die for our country
                    For totality of our country.

                              Majid Siraj

Kashmir is in the throes of change, a radical transition from an obsequious polity and feelings of nonentity in the society, to animated self-reliance and fervour to fight for a position in the world. People are torn between tyranny and freedom, peace and turmoil, hope and despair, living and dying, all at the same time!

Revolutions are not made by fate but by men. What drove them was the conviction that every man is master of his own salvation and the inherent responsibility towards their children and the country they live in.

In a few years from now this part of the book will be rendered obsolete. Kashmir will have been moulded into the shape of a pyramid, euphemistically speaking, with vestiges of civilisation still visible, or perhaps if wisdom prevails, we shall see a renascence of the lost paradise! We will consider the merits and drawbacks of all options possible but not available at this point in time. 'Independence' for Kashmir may only be a hypothesis, but out there the resolve to cherish it, is invincible and merits an attempt to configure possibilities. It may be relevant to quote some figures from a survey conducted by an Indian public opinion organisation called 'Mode' (October 18th, 1995, Outlook). 77% of the people want to decide their future outside of the Indian constitution. A plebiscite, if held, may reflect that poll, in which case the masses are intrinsically repressed under the present situation. The poll also revealed that human rights abuses by the forces have increased. Occupation by definition is complete. All decisions about the political status of Kashmir were peremptory, without either the prior knowledge or consent of the people and no matter if they were taken in Delhi or Islamabad. The basic rights of fourteen million members of world community are vitiated by the very people who underwrite them.

Here are some basic tenets of a framework for a solution.

1. It is the end of the road for the people's endurance. Any solution has to be durable.

2. All sections of the people will need to live in peace with each other. Minorities must live with dignity and a sense of security.

3. The final outcome must cease to be a bane for strife in the subcontinent. Any problems with peace between India and Pakistan will reflect directly on the lives of Kashmiris. Kashmir must act as a cohesive force for peace in the region.

4. Kashmir, as a place to visit, must not be closed to anybody from the subcontinent. The heartbreak of the exiled people or the frustrations for those wishing to visit Kashmir for religious pilgrimage, will stir passions.

5. Kashmir must be developed as a focus of attraction for visitors from around the world, and be seen to enhance the potential of the whole region.

6. Kashmir must not exist as an appendage, its people like a vassal community controlled by outside ascendant administration. That position will not work, as pro-active history has shown.

7. Kashmir must be seen to be neutral on the world political scene. This stance is central to its survival politically and economically. Kashmir has a vulnerable geopolitical situation and cannot get involved with regional polemic episodes.

8. The final outcome must provide for the resettlement of the two million of its people living as fugitives in exile.

9. The will of the people cannot be ignored. This is the most important of prerequisites. The wishes of scores of African nations smaller and less developed could not be bypassed in the decades when nationalism and self-determination were sweeping across continents. *Ultimately people are the masters*.

10. Defence of Kashmir is exigent because of its location. The British army kept a distance from Kashmir for that reason. Russian generals planned an invasion of Kashmir during the Tsarist rule. China, Mongolia and Afghanistan invaded Kashmir at different times and the southern borders have been violated repeatedly. A neutral army has to play a role in policing the borders. The composition could be debated and contingents from all South Asian countries could partake. Kashmir made a start at building an indigenous army called

the JK Militia, begun by Col. B.M. Kaul. It has since been merged with the Indian army. The hope is that further incursions will not take place. The political climate of the changing world is a saving grace for the region.

11. If a nuclear war erupts between India and Pakistan, it will be fought in Kashmir. The peace is fragile and politicians are unpredictable. Krishna Swami Sunderji, the last commander-in-chief of the Indian army described the Indian nuclear policy in allegorical terms: "Six blind men who cannot see the elephant, misinterpret the beast by touching its various parts." Ignorance about nuclear weapons in India may trigger off a devastating exchange with Pakistan. Resolutions of conflict in Kashmir may presage the end of the military race. Expensive nuclear programs may be expunged altogether from the subcontinent as a result.

Finality of accession to India as claimed by her politicians cannot be considered valid by the canons of international law. A status quo is not feasible, and negotiations have come to an impasse. UNCIP, the United Nations Commission for India and Pakistan, produced documents under a legal framework of UN guidelines with no compliance and an international court of justice failed to deliver a solution. What are the possibilities? Will Kashmir burn itself out? And the state of mayhem for the people persist and the world witness the remains of perdition? The future of Kashmir could be shaped in so many different ways!

(i) Jammu and Kashmir including Ladakh, Gilgat and Baltistan should become a part of India or Pakistan.

(ii) Jammu, Kashmir, Ladakh, Gilgat and Baltistan as a whole block should become an independent country. Leaders from Gilgat are campaigning for 'United States of Kashmir' with regional autonomy.

(iii) 'Ceasefire Line' converted into an international border; Kashmir divided between India and Pakistan. China to keep Aksia Chin and the Silk Road disputed areas.

(iv) The whole state be divided between India and Pakistan, except the Valley of Kashmir. The Valley annexed to some parts of Jammu and Ladakh, either as an independent country or having different degrees of accession with India or Pakistan. This solution has taken different forms of distribution of territory proposed by various politicians and world diplomats over the years.

(v) Jammu and Kashmir to become a confederation with India and Pakistan.

Sheikh Mohammed Abdullah, ex-chief minister of Kashmir, who was a key figure in the politics of Kashmir at that time, stated that his party formed a working group to study the solutions of the Kashmir problem. This was in 1953, when Pandit Nehru wrote to him, asking for this action to be taken before his departure to London for a conference on Kashmir. The working group members were chosen to be Bakshi Gulam Mohammed, Mohammed Syed Masoodi, Sardar Budh Singh, Girdhari Lai Dogra, Shyam Lai Saraf and Abdullah himself. The consensus resulted in the following:

* A plebiscite would be held in accordance with conditions agreed upon.

* Autonomy would be obtained for the entire state.

* Foreign affairs and defence would be placed under the joint control of India and Pakistan.

* The 'Dixon Plan' would be implemented along with autonomy of the region where the plebiscite is held. Bakshi was in favour of the Dixon Plan. The essence of his proposals were that Jammu and Ladakh would finally accede to India, Gilgit agency, Baltistan, districts of old Poonch Jagir and parts of Jammu in Azad Kashmir would accede to Pakistan. The Kashmir Valley including Muzafarabad was to be decided by plebiscite to join India or Pakistan. There was no proposal for complete independence in his plan.

Half a century has been lost with a lexicon of clichés exchanged as rhetoric and an indifferent response from the politicians of the world for whom their own vested interests are a prime factor. In the meantime, the destiny of the people in Kashmir hangs in the balance. I offered a grief-stricken family help with finding a refuge for their boys in another country. The father had been killed by the Indian army. "My two sons are very dear to me. They have lost their father, who died for a cause. We were born here and because it is our home, we will die here," was the curt reply of the bereaved widow.

A careful study of the events in Kashmir will reveal an outstanding feature. All world leaders including prominent Indian statesmen want the *people* of Kashmir to be the final arbiters in the dispute and yet it is these same people who are relegated a remote place on the political scene. The same people are manipulated, coerced, dehumanised, tortured and killed, all but shown any respect for their wishes. These are therefore sanctimonious revelations of politics, a far cry from the spectre of 'freedom' as the world knows it.

A quest for peace may for now culminate in frightening tides which hide the view of the yonder. The maelstrom will have to pass, before the twilight is visible.

It will become apparent from the sequence of events since Lord Mountbatten became involved in the dispatch of the Indian army into Kashmir, that an undercurrent of dissent was surging within the grass roots. Mr Abdullah became increasingly disparaged by India on account of the gradual erosion of his authority in administration and through a process of creeping substitution. His dream of Kashmir was fading away. His 'plebiscite front' party, was made illegal. The last convention of the party was held in Sopore (November, 1964). The Sheikh was not an active member of the front himself but all his close associates were running the campaign. That was the start of the troubles which have now become a vital constituent part of life in Kashmir.

148

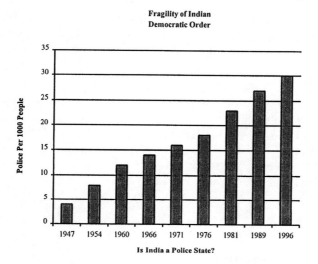

Fragility of Indian
Democratic Order

Is India a Police State?

A Disaffected Nation

We will study the past if we want to divine the future.

The people in Kashmir shared a glimpse of the emancipation sweeping across the world and progressively became aware of their underprivileged position and their rights. Fed up with their servile existence and the intrusive trespass upon their liberty, they came out to fight for their 'freedom.' The local administration turned upon them and force was used ruthlessly to govern Kashmir. This resulted in alienation from Indian rule.

Leaders like Sheikh Abdullah who controlled the hearts and minds of people at that time, did not, as it turned out, hold the reins of destiny for them anymore. Abdullah was coerced, jailed and he vacillated at crucial times for his survival. Many thousands of lives have perished, sucked into a political maelstrom created by unscrupulous politicians duelling for power.

Presence of the Military. The ubiquitous presence of a massive military force is perceived by the people as intimidation and an intrusion into their privacy. Kashmir is a small place. Army trucks in the thousands ploughing through the streets and village roads, day and night, make the state one large army camp. Intimidation and authority are forced upon civilians. The numbers of the military are excessive and year after year swell up into a formidable figure of 600,000; the largest occupational force in the world, equating to one soldier for every household in Kashmir. The army is reinforced by armed police derived from all parts of India. This appalling force was further reinforced by the most notorious of all Rashtrya Rifles (RR), now deployed all over Kashmir patrolling the interior of the cities and even camping in local police stations and private houses.

The first time people became conscious of the adversarial role of the Indian military was way back on a late summer afternoon in 1972, when the driver of an army truck started abusing a fruit vendor in Lal Choke, Srinagar. Local people gathered round and an argument ensued. The army truck returned to its base in Badami Bagh. Within half an hour truckloads of army personnel with hockey sticks in their hands tore through the city. They beat everyone they saw on the road. The physical damage was not significant but it became clear to the people that the Indian army in Kashmir were an alien malevolent force. Mr Abdullah, the Chief Minister, complained to New Delhi and got little response.

"By 1965 wherever you go in the valley a non-Kashmiri armed police is in evidence." (Prem Nath Bazaz, *The Crucible*).

Discrimination. Mr Abdullah as Chief Minister of Kashmir asked General K.M. Cariapa, the army chief of India why Muslims of Kargil (Kashmir) were denied entry into the Indian army. "Their loyalty to India is doubtful," was the reply. This was forty years ago when India was at peace with Kashmiris. The Indian administration have clearly demonstrated that Kashmiris are not a part of the populous of India. Telecommunications, airlines, the Inland Revenue, top IAS cadres and other Indian offices in Kashmir were openly 'no go' areas for the local people. They hand-picked a few relatives of political friends and honoured them with titles like IAS (Indian Administrative Service), a legacy from the British time – a title reserved for élite bureaucrats.

Economic Factors. The indigenous industrial base in Kashmir was eroded. Raw materials retrieved from natural resources were exported, leaving local developments undermined. Industrial subversion was a deliberate policy. Government quotas for copper, steel, plastic or any imported material were handed out as a political favour or given to people who were prepared to share the spoils surreptitiously. The prosperity in Kashmir has been like a whitewash of a crumbling house, the stalwarts taking the lion's share of the spoils.

Social Factors. The cultural mix of a Kashmiri with other people in the subcontinent is a slow process. The endearing sparkle and shiny faces of Kashmiris will stand out from thousands of others. The distinctive elocution of local languages means they speak other languages with an accent. It is impossible for a non-Kashmiri to pronounce all the syllables of the Kashmiri language. Students could not master the cadence and style of the language in a lifetime! Books taught in schools have been designed to deviate from local educational norms. The curriculum suitable for the Indian society as a whole, was not received favourably in Kashmir. The elders heard a different theme from their children, an alien philosophy and ostensibly a challenge to their own set of values.

Uncertain Future. I recall speaking to some friends, apparently opulent and successful businessmen, in a Srinagar club one night, way back in the 70s. I asked them about their investment in Kashmir. They all gave me a similar response. "We will possibly make a house here, so we can come back at some uncertain time in future, but investment on a serious scale is out of the question. Kashmir has no settled future. What is going to happen in a year's time? Who knows?" If I met them today, I know what they would say to me! Conditions got worse as time went by and made it difficult for any entrepreneurs to settle in and create something worthwhile to boost the image of their homeland. A sacrilege for Kashmir, plunged into a state of continuing attrition and denudation.

Religion. It may be fair to say that Indian rule in Kashmir did not affect the freedom of worship by people of any religion during normal times. It became nevertheless a common topic for concern that in schools, colleges and media, Indian culture was promoted.

Music. There was no control of local government over what went on the Indian sponsored TV or the radio. The viewing times were full of interminable matter about the virtues of an Indian lifestyle. Kashmiri music is the soul behind the life of the society and they heard it on radio and TV significantly vitiated and favourite songs warped. It was like playing *Lara's Theme* as *Jingle Bells*! Kashmir is a closed patriarchal society. People have a strong attachment to their root culture which precludes any easy change.

Hindu Reactionaries in India. The domestic politics in India strike at the raw edges of secularism and Hindutva. Hindu militants accuse Muslims as "Pakistani fifth columns" and subversive in nature. To them, Muslims in Kashmir are a blob in a sea of water, living in the Himalayan abode of Lord Shiva.

The propaganda from the Hindu Mahasaba and Jana Sangh was taking epoch proportions. They wanted the 'special' treatment given to Kashmir under article 370 to be scrapped and bring Kashmir in line with other states of India. The reactionaries used esoteric and uncivilised methods of gratuitous physical violence. Mr Jagmohan, member of the Upper House of India, (former governor of Kashmir), has postulated in his book *Frozen Turbulence* (very appropriately named) that, in order to bring an end to the agitation in Kashmir, a counter guerrilla force of a German GSG type should be deployed in Kashmir. The other part of his proposals was to impose a trade embargo on the Kashmiris. "Stop buying Kashmiri apples and carpets! The hardship will turn the people against the terrorists (freedom fighters) blaming them for the consequences." The ex-governor also wants to abrogate article 370 so that a large number of settlers, armed with guns, can be brought in from India and given land to build homes in Kashmir, (presumably ethnic cleansing would be easily achievable). "The first prerequisite is to establish authority on the ground," he has reiterated. It is five years now and the only authority established so far has been the conversion of the valleys of Kashmir into cataclysmic killing fields! The plan of action advocated by Mr Jagmohan fortunately did not become in total the Indian policy on Kashmir. India wants to solve the Kashmir problem in many respects more than Pakistan does. The problem is the 'Mexican stand-off'. No one wants to make the first bold move! The soft option is a stalemate. After all, it is the necks of Kashmiris on the line and they are dispensable, or so it seems!

The gradual erosion of the autonomy which began with the relationship of India with Kashmir was responsible for a loss of confidence and trust. Repression and mayhem were a consequence of the force applied to govern them.

Love and nostalgia for their relatives in Pakistan and the romance of an unseen entity of that country from the day of its birth, created maudlin feelings towards Pakistan. Kashmiris from the Valley have never seen what Pakistan looks like. Visiting Pakistan was controlled, and caused untold desperation.

All these factors combined with the revelation of their past servile status, made inroads into the minds of the people. Even a placid ascetic turned into a militant, resolute to offer any sacrifice for a change. No one would rest in peace and woe to the vanquished.

There are pertinent reasons why people from different parts of the state, across all physical boundaries, want to remain together and cherish a credible pluralist nation. These aspirations are multi-faceted and every aspect has a story to tell. Clubbed together the state represents an important symbol for the people of Kashmir. Kashmir existed as an independent nation up to the time the British relinquished their rule in India. India got its independence and was split into two dominions. Kashmir was caught up in a crossfire and for no fault of its people or even its rulers, got fragmented and enslaved, by an irony of fate, at the same time as the rest of the subcontinent achieved freedom!

Over many centuries, the culture, trade, art, and economy have been so intricately linked together between all parts of the state that their relationship seems, on the face of it, absolutely insuperable. The ring shawl culture of Kashmir would not be possible without the cashmere produced from the Pashmina goat specially reared for that purpose by the people of Ladakh. The beautiful rugs and woollen garments produced in Ladakh were admired by the people in Kashmir and sold in Srinagar for centuries. Tourists from all over the world complete their holiday of a lifetime only when they have combined Kashmir with Ladakh and Baltistan.

It is obvious to the people of Ladakh and Baltistan that, swallowed up by a large country, they will be a fringe community in a frontier border state. They will be living as servants to a large contingent of a resident army. The 80,000 people of Ladakh or an equal number in Kargil and other northern states do not wish to be marginalised as a dot in a gigantic country.

The Dogra population in Jammu have lived as descendants of the ruling family. They have a mindset whereby they consider their identity separate from Punjab. After all, it was Gulab Singh who put the state together in the first place, and fought against Ranjit Singh, the Punjab ruler. The Tawi River divides the beautiful city of temples into two parts before joining Chenab. It will be a sacrilege for the centuries-old bondage with Kashmir to be severed. The people of Jammu want to stay close to the rest of the state and continue as a host for the winter capital. They apprehend that the people from Punjab will consolidate their hold and finally Jammu will be annexed to Pathankot as an appendage and be a district of Punjab.

And as we write today, the agony of insecurity continues in this unfortunate land, caught in the fetters of power-politics and strife in which they are an innocent party.

Half a century has been lost in fighting fruitless deadly wars, verbal exchanges in the manner of a lexicon of clichés, the two rival countries slinging abuse at each other and a mute response from the politicians of the world. In the meantime, the destiny of the people in Kashmir remains in the balance and their roots are jostling from within for survival. We have to commend the people of Kashmir. They show a sense of solidarity, mutual dependence and a desire to share the vicissitudes of life. The masses are intrinsically close and help each other with food, shelter and a shoulder for comfort. They will not abandon their homes, come what may. A few bourgeois families have migrated. Comfort and avarice determined their circumstances.

A Case for Annexation to India or Pakistan

We must set out and make a case for the annexation of the state of Jammu and Kashmir to a dominion, be it India or Pakistan. The mainstay of this argument is described as follows:

1. Landlocked. Geopolitical factors.
2. Strategically vulnerable.
3. Economically unsustainable.
4. Geographically or historically a part of another country
5. Legally a part of another country.
6. Presence of occupation armies and laws of possession.
7. Factors domestic to India and Pakistan tied up with Kashmir.
8. Sentimental and cultural attachment.

1. Landlocked

Countries which are not landlocked have access to the sea. Kashmir has no sea on its borders but can communicate with all its neighbouring countries by land.

Kashmir may be landlocked, but, despite its gigantic mountains skirting round its perimeter as if to cradle it from harm's way, it has twenty-four routes in and out to the rest of Asia. Pamirs, the roof of the world separating it from Tajikstan, westwards from Afghanistan; Karakoram guarding the north-east from Tibet and China and southward from the Indo-Pakistan subcontinent. It was, with hindsight, a disadvantage to have arteries of communication into Kashmir. The repeated barrage of invasions would not have taken place! These difficult times, however, did bring in traders as well. Cashmere wool for the artisan community of Kashmir and all import and export of merchandise to China, Tibet, Afghanistan and India came through these routes.

Civilisations in isolation have, it may be argued, lost a lot as well as gained a lot with the confluence of populations. Kashmir needs an outlet into the world. Unfortunately, every country offering means of communication will only agree to do so by extolling a price in exchange.

2. Weak and Vulnerable

Kashmir is devoid of oil wealth or military capability. There are five big giants breathing down its neck and hovering over its domain. God is the only help close to the hearts of people. He will provide the stone of David to overcome the Goliath. Kashmir is like an ambrosial cake – too tempting to resist! And there are people ready to reach out and devour it. The most powerful have priority to claim ownership of the place and its people.

3. *Economically Unsustainable.*

In the present state of economy Kashmir will not survive on its own. It will not be able to support itself if every facet of its industrial base, productivity and enterprise are kept subdued. The people of Kashmir have always been praised for their ingenuity and their country for its resourcefulness. It is an important duty of all those who care to chronicle the events taking place, that Kashmir be seen as a self-reliant society. The future of Kashmir may take any form, it must be cogently reiterated that it is now a conviction with the people that they will abandon their existence as barnacles under ships carrying cheap American rice and handouts. Accepting gratis favours will presage obeisance and breed insurrection when ascendancy is claimed due to previous kindness.

Kashmir can earn significant foreign exchange. No figures have ever been published in Kashmir about how much the stock of forest and forest products have been worth. There are no recent published figures about produce from agriculture, horticulture or animal husbandry. People have reason to believe that all their resources have only been squandered and not exploited properly. The industries have vanished. It was common knowledge that money coming into Kashmir found a direct route into the pockets of the officials of the puppet regimes installed to keep political control. The incumbent ministers admitted openly that they were bent on the spoils for themselves and paid no regard to development. Kashmiris can live on crumbs! During curfews, they eat home-grown vegetables preserved by desiccation and painstakingly stockpiled. They have survived extreme weather conditions and political upheavals. They are not prodigal consumers and respect every grain of crop. They believe it is a sin to step on a grain of food, considered a blessing from God.

This land of plenty, like in olden times, can be an exporter of agricultural produce and many other products. The subject is dealt with in the chapter on the economy.

4. *Geographically and Historically a Part of the Subcontinent.*

In 1947, when British rule in India came to an end, the fate of Kashmir became an issue. Kashmir was not a part of British India, but the British resident in Kashmir represented British control of paramountcy, quite separate from their direct rule in India. As a result, the British could not allocate parts of the state to any dominion when they split the country between India and Pakistan. The prime minister of Kashmir and Maharaja Hari Singh wanted to stay independent. India and Pakistan both wanted annexation of the state to their dominion. Strife, intrigue and open wars resulted between the parties. The subject is discussed in more detail in the chapter on the history and the laws of Kashmir.

India claims Kashmir on the basis of secular philosophy of Indian democracy. The mixture of the Hindu majority, Jammu, the Buddhist majority, Ladakh, and the Muslim majority, Kashmir, becomes a showpiece of their ideology. The historical monuments of the Hindu religion in Kashmir are important landmarks of the faith and a reminder of the early days of their rule. There is a constant flow of pilgrims from all over India and they need free access into Kashmir. The road into Kashmir from India was updated, bridges built and even a railway link brought as far as Jammu. India also has access to the state through Himachal Predesh.

Pakistan, on the other hand, treats Kashmir as an integral part of its very existence. The partition was aimed at the Muslim majority places to join together to form Pakistan. Kashmir is more contiguous to Pakistan than India; the former has a highway into Kashmir which has the potential for a rail link, as against the treacherous cart road which connects India to Kashmir. They claim, geopolitically, that Kashmir is naturally a part of Pakistan.

5. *Legal Rights and Implications.*

India maintains that the instrument of accession signed by the Maharaja and later ratified by the Kashmir assembly makes the state an integral part of India. Pakistan rejects these claims. The Maharaja had abdicated his throne and was on the run. He did not have a mandate from his people to sign the accession to India. The signatures were obtained under dubious circumstances. The

Kashmir assembly was elected with a massive presence of occupying Indian forces still in the state and no chance of an impartial election. Legal details have been thrashed out in the United Nations by both countries and new legal points have been raised by resolutions passed by the United Nations and reports prepared by the United Nations' commission for India and Pakistan (UNCIP). The stark fact is that the issue remains unresolved and all the legal points have not been argued. The human rights violations and the consequences of occupation have overtaken the recurring polemic exchanges between India and Pakistan.

6. *Presence of Army and Law of Possession*

Armies get entrenched and an occupation is heralded. 'Possession is nine points of the law' applies in arguable situations, especially so in military occupation. The tentacles of an octopus have suckers at the end. In the depths of the sea, the suckers apprehend a prey. The law of nature allows the octopus to claim possession of the prey. It needs the food. This is biodiversity. The rule applies to all animal kingdoms. The armies have extracted a price wherever they have landed in the history of the world. The power of the gun is intoxicating. The captors decide that taking smaller species on is natural food for them. The natives of Kashmir are dispensable and have a secondary role to play in the laws which control them.

7. *Domestic Factors in India and Pakistan*

The incumbent governments in Pakistan and India are struggling to keep their democracies viable. Both have a slender majority in the parliament and depend heavily on having to co-opt minority parties. Kashmir is either used to stir up passions or to divert the people away from adversity. Kashmir is also in the firing line of abuse the two nations hurl at each other for whatever reasons! India has pockets of dissension in the north-east, the south of the country and Punjab. Kashmir gets the brunt of the blame wherever problems arise.

8. *Sentimental Attachment.*

It is an accepted fact that, if it were not the ancestral strings of attachment and maudlin feelings Mr Nehru had for Kashmir, he would not have acted with the zest he displayed in the events of October, 1947. It is a pity Mr Nehru was not a domicile of his ancestral country, Kashmir, at that crucial time, like R.C. Kak or P.N. Bazaz. He would have opted for a different course. It was very obvious he loved Kashmir but it seemed his concern for India was more important to him. Pakistan, on the other hand, found the receding ties with Kashmir tugging at her heartstrings. Kashmir, after all, was an integral part of the 'dream Pakistan'. The devotion to their sentiments was so great that both countries staked human lives and enormous resources, ruthlessly.

India or Pakistan?

Both countries have pleaded passionately that Kashmir is a part of their country. Both have produced arguments to support their perspective. The subcontinent has imploded into flames for half a century, resulting in unfinished business for the United Nations and a scourge on the 1.5 billion people of South Asia. Let us try and expound the genesis of the claims.

Case for Pakistan

Kashmir became independent when British paramountcy ended on August 24th, 1947. Pakistan was created with Kashmir as an important integral part. C. Rahmat Ali, in 1939, first started the Pakistan National Movement from Cambridge, England. He conceived the idea of the name Pakistan to mean 'pure country', but also to denote the first letters of Punjab, NWFP, Kashmir and Sindh federated into a sovereign state, 'Pakistan'. The British ruling contingent including Lord Mountbatten had allocated Jammu and Kashmir in their books to Pakistan. It was made clear by the incumbent British viceroy to Maharaja Hari Singh and his prime minister, Mr Ram Chand Kak, that the Muslim dominated state must accede to Pakistan. That was the basis of the two nation theory on which India was divided. Pakistan signed an agreement with the Maharaja's government to provide transport for the import of oil and salt etc., and postal and telegraph facilities as a prelude to final accession. Mr Ram Chand Kak, the Hindu prime minister of Kashmir, accepted Pakistan and offered a standstill agreement to Pakistan to give him time for terms of reference to be drafted. He was precipitously dismissed and replaced by pro-Indian Mehr Chand Mahajan.

Pakistan claims Kashmir as a part of its country, because it formed an important constituent of the total package offered to them when that nation was created. The geographical lifeline and the main arteries of communication with the outside world for Kashmir are also on the perimeters of Pakistan.

Both India and Pakistan maintain the other is the aggressor in Kashmir. Fortunately the people of Kashmir have not been implicated by either side, yet in this whole saga they are the main victims, suffering atrocities and an uncertain future.

Pakistan has denied acquiescence in the insurrection by Sudhans in Poonch against the despotic rule of the Maharaja and subsequent invasion of Pathans in support of the insurrection in 1947. It was in retaliation to the revolt by the Sudhans that the Maharaja's forces torched all the villages in Poonch. The flames could be seen from the hills of Murree in Pakistan! Following this, the entire Muslim population of Jammu, estimated at 500,000, were massacred and 200,000 of the remaining Muslims either fled into Pakistan or have remained untraced. Pathan's irruption into Kashmir was a result of these pogroms. The Sudhans have an Afghan ancestry and live on the left bank of the Jhelum River, while the right bank borders the Hazara district and NWFP. The conflict was a contiguous spillover. Pakistan was not implicated as alleged by India.

Pakistan has claimed that the people of Kashmir want to be a part of that country. The problem, of course, is that no one will know if there is any truth in that statement until a ballot box is offered to the people of the state.

Pakistan Has Challenged the Accession of Kashmir to India.

The reasons given are outlined and analysed below.

A. *A Premeditated Ruse.* India in connivance with Lord Mountbatten hatched a plot to annex Kashmir with India at an early stage. The plan was premeditated even before the invasion of the Pathans. The reasons generally promulgated by Pakistan can be mentioned briefly here.

1. Awarding three crucial Eastern Tehsils of Gurdaspur and the Zira districts, and Muslim majority areas to India was the first step. Cyril Radcliffe, the British engineer, was under directions from Mountbatten. Gurdaspur was the vital link between India and Kashmir. Christopher Beaumont, secretary to Sir Cyril Radcliffe, said in a statement: "Earl Mountbatten manipulated in India's favour the findings of the Boundary Commission." The award was not published until August 15th, 1947. There was little time for its implications to sink in.

   Two days before the award was finally announced, Mountbatten set up a special meeting over a sumptuous lunch with Radcliffe and a selected few. It was on this ill-fated occasion that vital 'link districts' were reallocated in favour of India.

   There were other Muslim majority places like Ajnala, Jalandhar, Nakodar, Ferozpore and Kasur allotted to India. Incidentally, not one Hindu majority district was included in the dominion of Pakistan, even if it was geographically contiguous with that country.

2. Early visits to Kashmir were made by Indian officials: Mahatma Gandhi, Mr Kriplani, the Maharajas of Patiala, Kupurthala and Faridcot. The plan for future action was being hatched. The subsequent dispatch of the Patalia regiments into Kashmir took place, even before October, 1947.

3. The construction of bridges and roads into India through Pathankot was expedited, replacing the established arteries of communication into Kashmir from Pakistan.

4. The surprise dismissal of Ram Chand Kak, prime minister of Kashmir, and his replacement by pro-Indian Justice, Mehr Chand Mahajan, who was the Indian member of the Radcliffe commission.

5. Lord Mountbatten set off for Kashmir with a 'memo' briefing him to "remove Kak, release Abdullah, Kashmir

to join constitutional assembly of India" (*Transfer of Power* 1942, Vol xi, No 229, pages 442 and 448).

6. The speed of deployment of Indian troops and aircraft carriers on October 27th when Kashmir was invaded was impossible to achieve in one morning. This was clearly planned far in advance.

7. Kashmir's post and telegraphs departments were in the hands of Pakistan in accordance with the agreement between the two governments. In the meantime, Indian post and telegraph services had already included Kashmir in their list of states, eight weeks before their army entered the state.

8. August 1947, Sheikh Abdullah was released from prison without any reason. He made a statement soon after his release in Huzuri Bagh, Srinagar that, "Only the liberated Kashmiri representatives will decide where to go and not the dominions. We must promote Hindu Muslim unity at this time when communal strife has torn India apart." In his exchange of letters on October 26th, 1947, the accession of Kashmir to India became a *fait accompli*. It was on October 30th, that Sheikh Abdullah was already head of the emergency government.

9. Sir Frank Messervy, Commander-in-Chief of Pakistan, stated that, "There is much evidence that the accession had been deliberately planned for weeks before the event."

10. On October 7th, 1947, Sardar Patel, Indian home minister, wrote to his defence minister, Mr Baldev Singh, that there was no time to lose, as reports were coming of an imminent intervention from Pakistan. The military assistance to the Maharaja must urgently claim the attention of the defence council. This was far in advance of the Maharaja consenting to dispatch the Indian army into Kashmir.

India did not make an immediate decision and could not have flown in two infantry battalions in one hundred planes within twenty-four hours. It can be safely said that the invasion of Kashmir had already begun far ahead of the events of 27th October, 1947.

B. *Pakistan Claims That the Instrument of Accession was Fabricated and Illegal.*

1. The Maharaja did not have a mandate from the people to decide their future on his own whim or even the consent of his own cabinet.

2. The Maharaja had already abdicated his throne. He was fleeing. He never returned to Kashmir after allegedly having signed Kashmir over to India.

3. All recorded statements of the Maharaja are against accession to India.

4. The signature on the instrument of accession from the Maharaja was either obtained under duress from an already frightened ruler or, as evidence has suggested, the signature was forged. The date on the document is supposed to be October 26th, 1947. The Maharaja was in Kud, midway between Kashmir and Jammu on that day, and Mr V.P. Mennon was in Delhi and could not possibly have obtained the signatures.

5. The document of accession has not been published or presented to the UN commissions. Does this paper even exist?

Pakistan has also challenged the resolutions passed by the pro-Indian Kashmir constituent assembly, endorsing the accession of Kashmir to India by the Maharaja. The elections in the state held with the overwhelming presence of the army and Indian armed police were fake and spurious and allegedly a meagre 2% actually voted.

Pakistan has made it clear to the people in Kashmir that as a part of Pakistan they will have a highway leading into Pakistan open round the year, and a railway link to the rest of their country and the subcontinent. Kashmiris will have access to jobs and opportunities like any other citizen of Pakistan. The rivers of Kashmir flowing into Pakistan will provide means for hydroelectric projects, irrigation, and exploitation of forest products with rivers acting as a means of transport. Tourism, trade and industry would be accelerated. The social mixing and interaction with the society in Pakistan would be free and warm-hearted.

Pakistan claims that the United Nations and the world assembly have over the years endorsed their view and resolutions were passed to start demilitarisation and a plebiscite in Kashmir but this has been stalled by India. The world governments have rejected the claim by India that Kashmir is theirs. The official maps in circulation round the world show Jammu and Kashmir as a separate state or as a disputed territory. A United Nations permanent presence in Kashmir since 1948 endorsed that view.

At the end of the day the mainstay of their claim on Kashmir is a vote from the people of Jammu and Kashmir. It remains to be seen.

The Case for India

The Indian side have made their points to back their convictions, pointing to their own political commitments to secularism and unity of their country. The events in the history of the remote past and the recent political status of Kashmir, where parts of Kashmir have been under their control, have all been used as reasons why Kashmir should be a part of India.

"In the minds of Mr Nehru and the congress, Kashmir is in miniature another Pakistan; if this nation can be successfully governed by India then the philosophy of secularism is vindicated." (Korbel, *Danger in Kashmir*, Princeton University Press, 1966).

India also fears Srinagar may hold Himalayan headwaters hostage, the source of Indus river tributaries which are essential for irrigation in most of Punjab and beyond.

India claims sovereignty over the state because the deed of accession to India was signed by the Maharaja of Kashmir and ratified by its elected constituent assembly. (The people of Kashmir have not accepted this accord as a final seal on their future and the future of their country. The Maharaja had no mandate to sign the instrument of accession and the assembly was not democratically elected and could not represent the wishes of the people.)

November 17th, 1951: Sheikh Mohammed Abdullah made a long speech in the Kashmir assembly making possibly the *best case for the annexation of Kashmir to India*. The salient extracts of the speech are stated:

1. Accession to India means that there is no danger of a revival of feudalism and autocracy.

2. During the last four years the government of India has never tried to interfere in Kashmir's internal autonomy.

3. The Indian constitution has set before the country the goal of secular democracy based upon justice, freedom and equality for all. This is the bedrock of modern democracy. This should meet the argument that Muslims of Kashmir cannot have security in India.

4. The Indian constitution has repudiated the concept of a religious state, which is a throwback to medievalist doctrine, by guaranteeing equal rights for all citizens.

5. Kashmir has been able to put through its 'land to tiller' legislation; is it possible that in alliance with landlord-ridden Pakistan with so many feudal privileges intact, that this economic reform will be tolerated?

6. The traditional markets for precious goods, arts and crafts from Kashmir has been centred in India.

7. India, being more highly industrialised than Pakistan, can give Kashmir equipment, technical service and materials. Potentially Kashmir is rich in minerals and raw materials for industry. Sugar, cotton and cloth can be obtained in large quantities from India.

8. An all-weather road link as dependable as the one Kashmir has with Pakistan does not exist. But this question has been studied and a stable system of communication is both feasible and easy. River transport for timber will be impossible except along the Chenab in Jammu which still carries logs to the plains. River transport is a crude system which inflicts a loss of some 20% to 35% in transit.

9. The presence of Kashmir in the union of India has been the major factor in stabilising relations between Hindus and Muslims of India. As a symbol of secularism Mahatma Gandhi referred to Kashmir quoting from the Bible: "I lift up mine eyes unto the hills, from whence cometh my help." (PS 121:1.)

10. Pakistan's claim of being a Muslim state is only a camouflage. Pakistan is not an organic unity of all the Muslims in the subcontinent. What will be the fate of one million non-Muslims in our state? As things stand at present, there is no place for them in Pakistan.

11. Another big obstacle is the lack of a constitution in Pakistan. The right of self-determination for nationalities is being consistently denied. We should remember Badsha Khan and Abdul Samad Khan and other fighters in Baluchisten.

12. The third course – of making ourselves an Eastern Switzerland – makes it difficult to protect our sovereignty and independence. We must have the goodwill of all our neighbours. What is the guarantee?

The main components of an Indian claim over Kashmir can be described as below:

1. The instrument of accession was signed by the Maharaja and endorsed by Mr Sheikh Abdullah the Kashmiri leader and his government.

2. The agreement was ratified by the constituent assembly of Jammu and Kashmir, an elected body representing the people of Kashmir.

3. Pakistan acquiesced in the invasion of the Pathans, in order to coerce the Maharaja to accede to Pakistan.

4. Pakistan infiltrated agents into Jammu and Kashmir to cause a Hindu-Muslim conflict.

5. Pakistan deliberately imposed an economic blockade in 1947, to force submission to accession. In this regard the gasoline, rock salt for which the people had a great weakness, wheat, oil and cloth were stopped. The postal system and banking facilities

were suspended. Pakistan has denied these accusations, stating that trucks loaded with goods were intercepted and plundered by Sikh rioters on a rampage.

6. The Indian government takes the view that as the acquisition of other states like Hydrabad, Junagarh, etc., was achieved, Kashmir should not be treated any differently. Pakistan's claim on Kashmir has no basis, *especially if they lost the state in the war*. The framework of the present Indian policy on Kashmir was laid down by Indira Gandhi. It was far removed from the ingredients of the policy publicised by her father, Mr Nehru. Her statements were cold but firm. "Indo-Pak relations are equated with Kashmir. Kashmir is not the cause but rather the consequence of India-Pakistan differences. It is too late to talk of a plebiscite, which was defined as the last stage of a sequence of events. The invasion by Pakistan in 1965 has destroyed the value of the UN resolutions. Ladakh is important to India for defence against China. We will not tolerate a second partition of India on religious grounds."

What do the other top ranking Indian politicians say about Kashmir? A few quotes will illustrate:

"When the Indian government is negotiating with the Nagas, it can also negotiate with Kashmiris. The Congress government has neglected all principals of democracy in Kashmir during the last decades." Prof. B. Ranga, Chairman, Swantantra Party of India (January 7th, 1967).

"Allow people of Kashmir to decide on a solution and accept their verdict." Mr J.P. Narayan, Saryodya party of India (January 10th, 1967).

"It was hypocrisy of the worst kind to keep saying that the Kashmir question had been solved." Mr G. Ramchandaran, Gandhi Peace Foundation of India.

It remains to be seen if the people of Kashmir will take all these factors as gospel and vote for their destiny with India. As a prelude to find the truth, they must get a plebiscite.

The Case for 'Independence'

"That this nation, under God, shall have a new birth of freedom; and that government of the people, by the people, and for the people, shall not perish from the earth."

Abraham Lincoln (November 1863).

In the long and eventful history of Kashmir, rulers like Ashoka, Lalityaditya and the great King Zain ul Abiddin, all heads of the country 'Kashmir' conquered parts of India, Tibet and China from Kashmir and annexed them to their kingdom.

People who lobby for 'independent Kashmir' equate independence with freedom. They quote:

Yet freedom, yet thy banner, torn but flying...
Streams like the thunderstorm against the wind...

(Byron).

This group of people believe that only self-rule will give them freedom. Says F.D. Roosevelt, "We look forward to a world founded upon some essential ingredients of human freedom and the first is the freedom of speech and expression." People in Kashmir have struggled for their right to free speech. Many thousands of lives have been lost and others have languished in prisons for a lifetime, for trying to exercise this basic right! The most important thing is freedom from fear and persecution, a luxury that Kashmiris have not enjoyed. They live with a constant sense of fear lurking in their minds about foraying invasions, violent repression, and are perpetually aware of a danger 'round the corner'. Children witness abuse and wanton exploitation of their elders, and find themselves caught in the political maelstrom as they grow up

The first task for all solution seekers is to make a case for changing the de facto political position of the state. The era of colonisation is past and buried. 1947 was the year of independence for the Indian subcontinent. That same year was also the year of the enslavement and division of the Kashmir state. The relationship with India had a run for half a century and it did not work. Reasons for a disaffected nation have already been described. It will suffice to reinforce the importance of the assistance to the state squandered by the puppet governments. There was a visible and vulgar flaunting of riches by the ruling families. People were kept ignorant about how much India was getting in foreign exchange earnings from tourism and exports from Kashmir or exploitation of natural resources such as forest products and minerals. No reports ever came out in the press about aid from international agencies like the IMF or the World Bank. Indian money circulated through government officials without any useful function being performed. A network of faithful politicians were supported by power and money. Honest officials were thrown out of service. One Pandit inspector of the water works department, I recall, somehow survived the sack. He became the famous 'honest Pandit' in Kashmir! Some people got used to the 'cash flow' situation prevailing and each small mercy was gratefully received. Mr Nehru was quoted as saying, "Only what goes in their stomach is lost!" The prime goal was to establish rule on the ground. Progress in real terms took second place. Fortunately, the people in Kashmir have the skills to survive and never had to forage for food, or sleep on the footpaths.

Political repression had reached epoch proportions. It was initially perpetrated by local governments installed by India and felt by people to be a continuance of older despotic regimes of the Dogras, only now even more reprehensible, because this time it was their own administration who inflicted misery on them. Torture was inflicted on prisoners by stubbing out lit cigarettes on faces, and jumping on stomachs with boots on. The victims were dubbed by the police as Pakistani fifth columnists and political activists.

Kashmir and India started off with a relationship in which only telecommunications, foreign affairs and defence were linked. Kashmir had a prime minister and its own devolved constitution. India eroded that status gradually and ruled by proxy from Delhi. The entry permit into Kashmir was abolished; IAS (Indian Administrative Service), and IPS (Indian Police Service), the cadre of Indian services, were introduced so that the Indian officers could be transferred into Kashmiri service. The census was now controlled from Delhi; the supreme court's jurisdiction extended into the state; Article 356/357 was applied to Kashmir wherein the president's rule could be extended. Article 248, dreaded by lawyers and introduced into Kashmir, made it easy to arrest a political activist under this Unlawful Activities act. This of course was replaced by the even more dreadful act – the TADA (Terrorist and Disruptive Activities (Prevention) Act).

The pointed end of these changes hurt local government chiefs. Their authority was diminished but for good reasons, pecuniary and political, they did not make a song and dance about the changes.

By now undercurrents of resentment against India were burgeoning. Mr Abdullah struck the final note in his speech in Hazratbal after Friday prayers. He was arrested soon afterwards. Pakistan has been accused of stirring religious sentiments and that the people of Kashmir based their revolt on religion. It is so unfortunate that each time the question comes up about unrest in Kashmir, Pakistan is blamed. The whole world has been made to believe that if it was not for Pakistan, the people of Kashmir would have been happy with Indian rule. The insinuation is demeaning for the people. They think they are capable of making their own decisions. They do not want to be seen to play the poodle to Pakistan. The extremist lobbies in Indian politics active in the wings have stipulated that India has been too soft on Kashmiris and not vigilant enough to ward off extraneous influences. It was up to the central government in Delhi to control how people in Kashmir behaved. They should have eliminated all detrimental factions in time. It may be said that whatever complacency has been shown to Kashmiris may have only put a lid on a boiling pot for a short time. The undercurrents were surging and the epicentre was in the core of the society.

The roots of disaffection in the society of Kashmir which culminated into this gratuitous demise of trust with India, was the massive presence of forces. The people of Kashmir have always loved to have people from all over the world as their guests and take delight in their company. The Indian army officers were housed in private homes as tenants and were respected. However, the numbers increased and open hostility surfaced. The presence of this formidable force on their doorsteps tore through the fabric of the society. They felt the sanctity of their homes was being violated. The concern was the treatment shown to the local public by members of the armed forces. It was common practice to find an Indian policeman coming into contact with a local person and hurling abuse.

Indian civil service officials were making their presence felt in large numbers. The airports, the telephone department, the Income Tax and Accountant General's departments became foreign territory for the locals. They visited these offices and saw no one who could understand their language or their problems. This was a dramatic change perceived for the first time in history.

Over many years the European visitors had always kept a different standard of relationship with the local trade and tourist industry. The choice of handicrafts was different, more expensive and top quality. The handicraft industry had to manufacture large scale rubbish to meet with the demands. They had to compromise on their taste of selection of design and service.

A holiday in Kashmir was the cheapest in the world! The Western tourist traffic was dwindling every year. Shanties and Indian style cafés in Gulmarg and Pahalgam sprung up to cater to the needs of Indian visitors. The geography of the beauty spots changed. The roads turned into a dusty hell, studded with murky potholes. Bridges were crumbling away, the exuberant and radiant charm of the mountains eroded in a discreet manner, as if a conspiracy was being hatched to vandalise Kashmir.

It remains to be seen if the future events take cognisance of the needs of Kashmir and its people, or will the power of the big nations swing the tide?

How important is it for the world community to save Kashmir from perdition?

LEGAL STATUS OF KASHMIR

Hanging in the Balance

Retro-active laws prevailing in British India in 1947 and international courts over the years, can be seen today to greatly underwrite the status of Kashmir as 'disputed', whose polity *de jure* remains undecided.

Any constitution or laws governing certain legal rights of people is referred to as the 'Magna Carta' of that constitution. India has been a high profile advocate of the charter. It may seem ironic, but on March 16th, 1994, when the prime minister of India, Mr Narasima Rao, visited Runnymede in England to commemorate the Magna Carta, three youths were apprehended in Kupwara, Kashmir, and executed at about this time. The Magna Carta, the great charter of liberties forced out of the teeth of King John by barons at the time, has become the basis of the rights which individuals of Kashmir have come out to seek.

They have a strong case to demand to be heard and use the citizens' charter which guarantees basic human rights. It would be sheer perjury for anyone to uphold the view that the people of Kashmir have chosen their fate and exercised their franchise.

In a repressive regime, laws can be tailor-made to impose authority. An interesting parable has flashed through my mind: A farmer plants an iron grid to restrain cows from escaping. The cows have small feet which will fall through, if they try to cross it. The farmer himself can walk without any problem. He made a 'law' for the cows and cows have to obey or face the consequences of getting trapped. The farmer need not consult the cows. He owns them and they are inarticulate.

Any legal actions felt necessary to be taken against Kashmiris were preceded by making laws to suit the particular occasion. There were no formalities observed and no constitutional democratic process involved.

In order to epitomise the freakish nature of the laws practised in the land, I am reminded of two events. Early August 1953, the Kashmiri government's law secretary, a friend of mine, went into hiding. He surfaced after two days, but much later on told me in confidence that he had been working on a draft amendment to the Kashmir constitution without sleep for two nights. It was now legal for Karan Singh, the Maharaja's son, the Sadri Riyasat to arrest Sheikh Abdullah, the serving prime minister of Kashmir, while he was still in office. The 'Lion of Kashmir' was promptly put in his cage!

During early 1989, Farooq Abdullah, chief Minister of Kashmir, said on News Track (India): "If Shabir Shah, the militant leader, is released by the court again, I will have him arrested for another offence round by the other side." The Shah's incarceration was guaranteed. He spent 20 years of his 40 years of life in prison without any redress by the so-called 'law'.

'Laws are made to be broken' – a cliché often quoted in legal circles and these broken laws become bread winners for the lawyers. In Kashmir, laws have only been made to be broken! In the name of law and order the masses can be coerced into being a compliant society and thus controlled. The demagogues use laws as a weapon to exercise authority.

Stalwarts of international law claim that the accession of Kashmir to India will stand in scrutiny. On March 22nd, 1942, Sir Stafford Cripps on orders from prime minister Winston Churchill, made it clear in his draft resolution that the states will stay out of the union and enjoy the same status as the Indian union. Mr Rajagopalchari accepted the ruling, but other Congress leaders rejected it. King George V proclaimed his "determination ever to maintain privileges, rights and dignities of the princes of India"... "The princes may rest assured," he declared, "that the pledge remains unimpaired and inviolable." The pledge was broken while his emissary, Mountbatten was still holding office as Governor General of India. Hydrabad, Junagarh, and Kashmir were de facto independent states. All three were invaded. An act of malfeasance in the face of international laws.

The Indian Independence Act of July 17th, 1947 passed by the British parliament gave birth to the two dominions, India and Pakistan. The same act, section 7(b), ended paramountcy over Kashmir (including all Indian states) making the state by default a free entity. Unfortunately, the British also allowed the autocratic Rajas the right to accede to India or Pakistan or remain independent. (Section 2(iv)). Maharaja Hari Singh was free to choose the future of his state. The Indian government has stated that the Maharaja exercised his right and acceded to India on October 26th, 1947. On the present evidence it is by no means clear that the Maharaja ever did sign an instrument of accession, or if he did, whether his signatures were obtained under duress. If that is the case, the Indian forces must be treated as a guest army in Kashmir. It may be that the instrument of accession did exist, in which case it becomes mandatory to consider it in its totality. If any part of this contract document has been breached, then the whole agreement is null and void. An important clause in the document stated that the accession was left for the people of Kashmir to decide through a plebiscite as soon as conditions permitted. Technically speaking, if the accession did not take place (conditional though it was) Kashmir would be a free country, even today. The reasons given to challenge the authenticity of the instrument of accession are as follows:

1. The Maharaja writes to Lord Mountbatten on October 26th, 1947, allegedly asking for military aid in return for accession to India. Lord Mountbatten accepts his terms and his request for military aid in a letter dated October 27th. The instrument of accession was supposed to have been signed on October 26th, a day before the reply came.

2. The Maharaja could not have put signatures on any document on October 26th because he was travelling by road, with his possessions, from Srinagar, Kashmir to Jammu and spent the night in Kud.

3. Mr V.K. Menon, the senior Indian diplomat negotiating the accession, and Mehr Chand Mahajan, prime minister of

Kashmir, were both in Delhi on the 26th. Mahajan was representing the Maharaja. Menon could not physically have been in Jammu to witness the signature of Maharaja on the accession document.

4. It was 10 a.m., on October 27th, when Menon and Mahajan set off from Delhi for Jammu and that afternoon is the first time the Maharaja knew about the decisions taken by the Indian government. By this time every available aircraft laden with Indian army troops had already landed in Srinagar.

5. The accession document (C) has not been circulated in its legitimate form. The doubt still remains, if the document ever existed. A recent report published by *Asian Age*, September 2nd, 1995, quoted the Jammu English weekly the *Sahogi Times* as stating that the original accession document signed by Maharaja Hari Singh and Lord Mountbatten is missing from the state archives. An unlikely event! Was it there in the first place is the question people are asking.

6. The Maharaja had demonstrated to India that he was not willing for Kashmir to accede to India. The irony of the matter lies in the fact that it was only Mr Ali Mohammed Jinnah, the Governor General of Pakistan, who said that the Maharaja was entitled to remain independent. Mountbatten and Mr Nehru rejected that option for him.

In conclusion, an inference can be drawn that the Indian army had already entered Kashmir and were fighting the Pathans in Srinagar, when the Maharaja may have been given the document of accession to sign. The only comfort offered to him was retention of his son as constitutional head. This was a late stage for Maharaja to have any opinion in the matter. Even if he did sign under duress, his land had already been violated by forces from India and the Pathans.

Having control of the state of Jammu and Kashmir, the Indian administration put a legal framework into it. Lord Mountbatten and Mr Nehru maintained that a plebiscite would take place and people would finally decide their future. In the meantime, Kashmir was brought within the envelope of the Indian constitution, except in part XXI of the constitution wherein a special provision was made for Kashmir. It was under the 'Temporary and Transitional Provisions' that the accession was confined to the defence, foreign relations and certain aspects of the communications. This became the 'Article 370'. Clause (3) of the article clearly stating that the President of India may by public notification declare that this article shall cease to operate.

Article one of the Indian constitution states that Kashmir is a part of the Republic of India as of January 26th, 1950. The instrument of accession will be a thing of the past in the new constitution and full integration with the Federal Republic of India does not need that instrument. That brings us back to the 'Farmer and his cows' story!

Article 370

Mr Gopalaswami Ayyanger, the Indian diplomat, was answering questions about special status and Article 370. He said, "Kashmir's conditions are special and require special treatment. In the first place there has been a war going on... part of the state is still in the hands of rebels and enemies. We are entangled with the United Nations in regard to Jammu and Kashmir. We cannot tell when we shall be free from this entanglement. That can only take place when the Kashmir problem is satisfactorily settled. Again, the Government of India has committed itself that an opportunity will be given to the people of the state to decide for themselves whether they will remain with the Republic or wish to get out of it."

The enticement of the leadership of Kashmir to accept a semi-autonomy in a quasi-federal orientated policy towards India was readily taken up by the opportunist upstarts in power.

Article 370 was adopted and put in part XXI of the Indian constitution as 'Temporary and Transitional provisions.'

The natural law in India is to get possession and then argue its legality. *Nine points of the law* are already won! Promulgation of the Disturbed Areas Act in July 1990 was specially enacted for Kashmir, and only 20 Kilometres of Poonch and Rajori in Jammu, the rest of Jammu was spared. The Indian army now had legal support for open play in the killing fields of Kashmir.

The Indian constitution has been framed to portray the values of a republic society, and democracy. The Panchsheel tenants were circulated for peace and harmony at home and abroad. 'Panchsheel', or five principles of peaceful coexistence, formed the basis of the agreement with China over Tibet. They were; 'mutual respect for each other's' territorial integrity and sovereignty, non-aggression, non-interference in each other's internal affairs, equality and mutual benefit and peaceful coexistence. Article 51 of the constitution states that 'International commitments' must be honoured. The UN charter is clear that Kashmir is disputed. India does not honour the position taken by the international community. That is one striking example of how India does not respect its own constitution.

Incursions from Delhi

The temporary accession of Jammu and Kashmir with India put in place by Mountbatten and Mr Nehru was promptly declared to be limited to defence, communications and foreign affairs, and subjected to a plebiscite. This article of faith and legal commitment was soon forgotten.

1958. Indian Administrative Services were Incorporated. It was decided that instead of having to repeal article 370 that the aim could be achieved by extending to Kashmir, in successive stages, all those articles of the constitution which did not apply to the state. The article 370 would be eroded.

1959. The census control extended from Delhi. This gave updated information about what was happening with the various ethnic groups in order to control their allegiance to Indian rule.

1960. The supreme court's jurisdiction was extended to Kashmir. This mainly affected the political prisoners. The local high courts could not be relied upon to pass judgements on all the thousands of political activists languishing in jails.

1961. The development of the industries was taken over by the central government. This especially applied to forest-based industries and the exploitation of natural resources. It would, for instance, not be possible for a local person to start a paper mill without the approval of the central ministry in Delhi.

December 4th, 1964. Articles 356-357 were applied to Kashmir. Laws applicable to the state would now be made in India.

High courts, trading corporations, and the price control organisation would now be controlled from Delhi. Elections would be held in the Kashmir assembly to appoint a member to central parliament in India.

December 27th, 1964. Presidential rule could now be promulgated in the state.

1965. Central labour laws were now effective in the state. This had political implications. The handicraft industry being run from home and all family members partaking of the work – laws could enforce a clamp down on this industry if only as a tool to keep people subverted.

1966. The state of Kashmir was now permitted to elect members to the Indian parliament 'Lok Sabah'. The members were hand picked and Kashmir was now represented, just like any other state of India.

1969. Article 248 including the Unlawful Activities Act was promulgated.

1975. The Kashmir Accord was signed. Article 370 could now be abrogated at any time by the president of India by virtue of Article 254 of the Indian constitution.

1989. The infamous TADA or Terrorist and Disruptive Activities (Prevention) Act was extensively used in Kashmir to justify human rights abuses and the incarceration of many thousands of young people in Indian prisons. A modern coliseum harbouring hungry lions, and anyone can be thrown in!

The metaphor of the 'camel in the desert' story can be applied to Kashmir! "The sun is too hot. Can I just put one foot inside the tent?" the camel said to his master. "So kind of you sir, my second foot is a little hot. Can I put my neck in for a while?" Not enough room in the tent – the master found himself out in the sun, and the camel was inside. It is very clear that India has come a long way from the October 1947 agreement with the Maharaja and subsequently the Delhi agreement with Mr Abdullah.

There is colossal circumstantial evidence of the disputed political status of Jammu and Kashmir.

1. The hard core of the leadership after the inception of Home Rule and the nascent democracies of the two republics are on

record to have declared that Jammu and Kashmir state is not annexed to India or Pakistan. The statements are sealed and stamped in all the pending files of Kashmir. Lord Mountbatten was the Governor General of India when he clearly reported to the British government that the possibility of the accession of Kashmir would have to be ascertained by its people's wishes through a plebiscite, therefore Kashmir was intrinsically disputed, even after November 1947.

Mr Jawaharlal Nehru, Mahatma Gandhi, Mr Jayaprakash Narayan and many other top leaders of India have stated to the world that a plebiscite will be held and the people will decide which dominion they will choose to accede to. The premise was that Kashmir is not already a part of any country. The steel-willed home minister of India, Sardar Patel, was in no doubt that Kashmir would accede to Pakistan. The Pakistani leadership has always maintained that Kashmir, including Azad Kashmir, are disputed and politically undecided. No judicial forum in the world will vitiate evidence as positive as these statements.

2. *The United Nations* and its council and general body have a definite position on Kashmir. Jammu and Kashmir are disputed and their status, undecided. The political maps show it and all the files on Kashmir are manifestly clear. The resolutions still pending on Kashmir have all maintained the premise that the status of the state is undecided. The UNCIP representatives deputed to solve the Kashmir dispute and their proposals for settlement all clearly show Kashmir as undecided. India accepted the essence of the resolutions, which was a 'reference to the people of Kashmir'. India wanted Pakistan to vacate their army first. The people of Kashmir in the meantime were waiting for these arguments to be resolved.

Part 3, paragraph 1 of the UN Resolution August 13th, 1948 states: "the Government of India and government of Pakistan reaffirm that the future status of Jammu and Kashmir shall be determined in accordance with the will of the people." Kashmir cannot, therefore, be a part of *any* country.

UNCIP Resolution of January 5th, 1949 again stated, *"The* accession of the State will be decided through the democratic method of a free and impartial plebiscite." Soon after having accepted that resolution the Indian generals met their counterparts from Pakistan on January 18th-27th, 1949, in order to draw the lines of a ceasefire through Kashmir. The people were soon forgotten, having served their purpose of political expediency.

The UN Resolution of September 20th, 1965 after the war ended and the ceasefire was accepted, it was stated that steps should be taken towards a settlement of the political problem underlying the conflict. Kashmir was the bane and its disputed nature was emphasised.

A critical analysis of why the UN has failed to implement its resolutions in Kashmir.

Boutros Boutros Ghali, the United Nations Secretary General, said recently that the resolutions on Kashmir are 'political' in nature and cannot be enforced. In order to implement the resolutions a different instrument will have to be put in place.

The resolutions came to an impasse de facto by inaction on the political front. India and Pakistan did not show any signs of resilience, or co-operation with the UN in solving the problem. Indian and Pakistani forces were fighting a war during that time and the United Nations were deliberating on the various ways to resolve the conflict. The natural tendency of either government was to stymie progress if they found that their army had made an advance. A *military solution* would have put a seal on the fate of Kashmir, according to Mr Bajpai, the head of the Indian delegation at the UN. "A plebiscite will not be an option," he said. The UN Resolution of January 20th, 1948, was passed by the security council by a vote of nine, with the USSR and Ukraine abstaining. A three-member commission was appointed to investigate the complaints of India and Pakistan and a report of the situation from the subcontinent. There was no mention of the withdrawal of troops or a plebiscite in this resolution.

The UNCIP (United Nations Commission For India and Pakistan) worked hard for over three years to bring about a resolution. They failed.

1. India wanted Pakistan to be treated as an aggressor, and did not agree to proposals of demilitarisation and a plebiscite. The Indian position was that the Kashmir assembly, headed by Sheikh Abdullah, would hold the proposed plebiscite and confirm or reject their accession to India.

2. Pakistan's position was that the invasion of tribals from NWFP into Kashmir was without their knowledge and proposed to help India and the UN to make them withdraw. The Pakistani army had to get involved when the Indian army were threatening their own borders. They maintained that all armed forces from both countries would pull out before a plebiscite was held under UN auspices.

The resolution of April 21st, 1948 was not implemented for the following reasons:

1. India and Pakistan did not use Article 96 of the charter. This would enable the UN to ask for the opinion of the international courts of justice to determine if the accession of Kashmir to India agreed by the Maharaja was legal. If the decision was yes, then it would be right for India to accuse Pakistan of being an aggressor. If the decision was a negative, then both countries were occupying foreign territory.

   This course of action was not taken by India and Pakistan because of the uncertainty of what the decision would be and that their claim to Kashmir may have been jeopardised.

2. Chapter VII of the UN Charter was also not used. This gives the UN power to intervene in case of an impending war. The fact is that Indian and Pakistani armies were already in combat and they both chose not to use the charter. It would have enabled the UN to clearly define the aggressors and their designs. The Council could have taken measures to enforce its decision.

3. The USSR factor played an important role. The UN was aware that any strong resolution which was enforceable would be promptly vetoed by the USSR. The feeling was that the USSR was not interested in any solution to the

problem, certainly not if the USA and Great Britain were supporting. Both the latter countries were accused by India of playing a partisan role in favour of Pakistan.

Kashmir became incorporated into the cold war and the cold war was incorporated into the issue of Kashmir. India played with finesse on the world scene and declared a policy of 'Non-alignment'. George Washington, commenting on this political stance stated that it was a "prescription for serving one's interest by remaining aloof from the quarrels of others [superpowers] and profiting from their distress. The two are not mutually exclusive. In international politics, the enemy's enemy is a friend." In fact, India was leaning on the red block all the time. It was only with Eastern Europe that India had a balance of trade surplus. The USSR sold arms to India and supported them openly in Kashmir. An important factor for Indian recalcitrance at the UN. In turn, India did not censure the USSR in its suppression of the Hungarian revolution in 1956, or its invasion of Afghanistan in 1979, a country so close to India.

4. Chapter VI of the charter used by India to lodge the complaint has limited powers. It enabled the UN to mediate, negotiate, reconciliate and arbitrate. This is the chapter used by the parties in the Kashmir dispute. No decisions are enforceable.

5. India did not want to internationalise the dispute. The UN appointed Admiral Chester Nimitz as an arbitrator and he was supported by President Truman of the USA, and Lord Atlee of Great Britain. His arbitration was accepted by Pakistan but rejected by India.

6. *UNCIP.* The UN Commission for India and Pakistan went through a protracted ordeal of negotiations, so that even in March 1949 they were still working on their proposals. This period was too long and the attitudes of the politicians in the subcontinent became hardened. The ceasefire line in Kashmir became a feature. The line was monitored by United Nations observers. The UN opened an office in

Srinagar and Muzafarabad. In a way, the UN presence over the stand-off position helped to perpetuate the partition of Kashmir and its political status.

7. The UN resolution of March 14th, 1950, was carried by eight votes with two abstentions, India and Yugoslavia, and the USSR (boycotting the Security Council at that time). The resolution, based on the proposals of General A.G.L. McNaughton of Canada, the president of the council, stated that there be a "simultaneous demilitarisation by both India and Pakistan to a point that no threat of war presented across the border." (Paragraph two). The resolution gave five months for this to be achieved. The UNCIP was replaced by an arbitrator. India and Pakistan agreed. In the event, Sir Owen Dixon, an Australian jurist was chosen to represent the UN. His mission failed because India rejected the idea of gradual demilitarisation as contained in the resolution. Sir Owen made proposals such as to have a neutral administration in Kashmir and Azad Kashmir. This was rejected by India. He then proposed a regional plebiscite. This meant partition and India and Pakistan taking regions who vote for them. Pakistan accepted a partition only if the Valley was included with Pakistan. India rejected the proposal. Sir Owen returned and, having failed, recommended to the council to keep their "hands off Kashmir and let the parties decide for themselves."

8. February 21st, issue, the Security Council met again to debate the Kashmir issue, now coming to boiling point. On March 21st, 1951, a draft resolution was presented by the USA and Great Britain. It was affirmed that the previous resolutions of August 13th, 1948 and January 5th, 1949, were accepted by India and Pakistan on the issue of a plebiscite. Once again the resolution passed contained: (1) the appointment of a UN representative; (2) demilitarisation and (3) arbitration if mediation failed in three months. It was carried by eight votes.

The USSR and Yugoslavia were not present. India abstained on a legal point of being a party to the dispute

(Article 27). Pakistan accepted the resolution and India rejected it, because of the 'arbitration clause.'

The UN appointed Dr Frank Graham, an experienced politician from North Carolina, to try to effect demilitarisation, which was a prerequisite for a plebiscite. He put forth many proposals but eventually when it came to the crunch the Indian government accepted demilitarisation to the extent of having 21,000 armed forces, and Sheikh Abdullah's government, and in Azad Kashmir complete demilitarisation with 2000 local forces, and 2000 unarmed civilians who were refugees. Pakistan accepted these proposals and the security council passed one more resolution on December 23rd, 1952.

9. The resolution urged India and Pakistan to agree the proposals and comply within 30 days. India refused to comply. Pakistan accepted the resolution. The negotiations were resumed in New York and then in Geneva in February, 1953. The fact remains that the impasse on demilitarisation has never been overcome.

Tashkant Declaration of January 10th, 1966. The heads of the Indian and Pakistani governments agreed to stop waging war against each other, to exchange POWs and withdraw to the 1965 borders. Apart from the rhetoric of exchanging goodwill and trade, the agreement was signed to continue to meet at the highest levels in order to discuss the outstanding problems. These meetings never took place. It is said widely that Mr Lal Bahadur Shasti, the Indian PM, had agreed to a solution of Kashmir with Mr Z.A. Bhuttoo, the president of Pakistan. No one will know the truth. Mr Shastri, unfortunately for Kashmir, did not live long enough to speak.

The position held by the international community, including major political organisations and world leaders, is unanimous about its policy on Kashmir. The official stand on Kashmir is a 'disputed country', and by implication it is not considered as a part of India or Pakistan or China. No world leader on official visits to India or Pakistan, except the Russians, have ever visited Jammu and Kashmir. The invitation was given to the British royal family

and ministers and other heads of states. It was promptly declined.
A visit to Kashmir would endorse the Indian policy on Kashmir.

Apart from the United Nations' official stand on the disputed status
of Jammu and Kashmir, the world's major governments have
declared that the sovereignty of Kashmir is undecided. Kashmir
therefore is not a part of India or Pakistan.

United States Department of State Bureau of Public Affairs,
Washington DC July, 1994, stated: (2) "This member includes the
Indian state of Jammu and Kashmir. The United States considers
all of the former princely state of Kashmir to be disputed territory.
India, Pakistan and China each control parts of Kashmir.

USA Washington DC Congress. Honourable J Kenneth Blackwell
in a briefing paper (January 1994) states on violent repression in
Kashmir, "This is not a civil war because India's occupation of
Kashmir has never been accepted by the international community."

British Foreign Office, London. Under Secretary of State Tony
Baldry writes on 30th March, 1994, "The status of Kashmir has
been in dispute since India and Pakistan became independent."

Like a lot of world leaders, Premier Chou En-lai of China said on
September 19th, 1965, that his government "gives all-out support
to the people of Kashmir in their struggle for self-determination,
which they have been perfidiously deprived of by India."

The puppet regimes installed by India in Kashmir have never had a
credible mandate from the people to ratify their accession of
Kashmir to India. The elections they held were spurious. I will
relate one example. Working as a district medical officer, I was
given verbal orders to instruct employees from all over the district
to travel to the capital city on election day, and if required, cover
themselves with a veil and cast votes. Curious as to why a veil
was necessary, it was explained in confidence, that men are
marked with ink on the right hand when they vote. Women are
marked on the left hand. The same man can vote twice. They
will all be given fake names. I refused and met my fate. I was
transferred to a less important post. The district commissioner
taking me into confidence told me how he had got two people
kidnapped for two days. They were supposed to nominate and

second a rival political candidate. He burnt the nomination papers and claimed he had never received them. The young people saw corruption hitting them in the face everywhere. The malady was channelled into the community. These rulers played dirty politics with the people for personal gratification. They were partly responsible for the intractable impasse and half a century of misery for the people! They could have played a constructive role and brought sound realities to bear upon the authorities in India and Pakistan. They found comfort in closing their eyes and enjoying the tenuous benefits. That attitude by these people was positively harmful in the history of Kashmir, and created false hopes and expectations in the minds of the Indian leaders. The result was that India got more and more deeply involved, spent more money and effort and lost some men from their army. In other words, in the absence of a local government, Kashmir would be ruled from Delhi and Delhi would have been directly responsible for infractions, and defiance in the face of international laws.

November 20th, 1951. The Jammu and Kashmir Constitution Act was passed by the Kashmir assembly. Maharaja Hari Singh was stripped of all his powers. Kashmir was now an autonomous state except for its defence, foreign affairs and communications. That status has never held, making the resolution invalid.

The position taken by India in international forums also supports the disputed nature of Kashmir. There is a pro-active debate on at all levels, in the Central Treaty Organisation, the South-East Asia Treaty Organisation, the Organisation of Petroleum-Exporting Countries and the UN. In December, 1962, India and Pakistan held talks on Kashmir in Rawalpindi, Delhi, Karachi and Calcutta. India offered 1,500 square miles of Kashmir to Pakistan. Pakistan was prepared to let India keep areas adjoining Himachal Predesh. One solution proposed by India was a 'Quadrangular Union' confederation between India, Pakistan, East Bengal and Kashmir. The crucial evidence is that Kashmir was a separate entity. The talks held with Pakistan as recently as in 1994 had Kashmir on its agenda. Simla Agreement talks have been offered to Pakistan through all international political forums. A limited autonomy has been discussed with some leaders in Kashmir. India could not have discussed Kashmir consistently for all these years, if it was an integral part of that country. Surely all the evidence points clearly to the undecided status of Kashmir and no argument can beguile the world that the question of the future status of Kashmir remains settled!

India's relations with Kashmir from the beginning showed a distinct pattern. It was a meeting of two strangers. Initially a friendly induction time, it was soon followed by a sense of alien occupation. The pattern of despotic malevolent rule was construed as 'occupation' or 'seizure, as by invasion' rather than a union of two partners. The first contact ever between the two was made by the Indian army ground troops, airlifted from Delhi. They fought two wars with Pakistan and one with China on Kashmiri soil.

People were treated as a nonentity. They remonstrated to vindicate the prima face case of deception by the Indian administration in having reneged on their promise of a plebiscite. The people felt they were held hostage to peremptory sanctions, a position not tenable in a democracy. Civil liberties were nondescript. Instead, alongside the regular army, the Indian armed police forces were deployed *facing* the civilians of Kashmir, from the very beginning. The numbers of both forces has mounted up every year to half a million, one sixth of the total of the Indian army. The veracity of this relationship lies in a retroactive odyssey of hostilities between the people and the forces when they come in contact with one another.

India is using brute force to subvert Kashmiri people to accept occupation as a final solution for their future. They give the dog a bad name and label it. People are accused of breaking their laws. *You cannot draw up an indictment against a whole people.*

A conclusion can be drawn from all the evidence stated, and supported by dossiers on record, that the political and legal position of Kashmir is contentious and *hanging in the balance.*

It is the belief of many hundreds of prominent people of India, Kashmir, and the world, that the status of Kashmir be treated as undecided and on that premise the presence of Pakistani, Indian or Chinese administrations in parts of Jammu and Kashmir be treated as illegal. The present political status has been forced upon people as peremptory and cannot be justified.

SCRIPTURES

Forgive me yes, forget me not

These are the events engraved in my heart

Beautiful children of Kashmir for a time lived a happy and gregarious life. The last five years have thrown them into a tempest, taking away their smiles, freedom and security. They are chased through alleyways, marauded and killed. They have witnessed blood and tears all through their years of growing up. Their classrooms and playgrounds have become battlefields. These children now see a future of death and destruction staring them in the face. Many thousands of parents have returned their children to earth as martyrs of the nation.

I would like to pay them a tribute and offer laurels to the valiant.

'Amaranthine Accolade'

For Those Young Faces
The Children Of Heaven
Audacious, stupendous and mighty proud
They laid down their lives for the nation they loved
Unfettered and Brave the message they gave
We lie down as martyrs, for the honour we save!
Beloved heroes, forever live on
In the history of Kashmir for those unborn

Majid Siraj

"The child's one chance to grow properly in mind and body should be shielded from the mistakes, misfortunes and malignancies of the adult world. This protection should have the first call on society's concerns." So it stated in the 'Progress of Nations' report (UNICEF). It is normal to see boys dashing in panic, jumping over fences into people's gardens to run away from the advancing forces? They are fear-stricken and have nightmares at night.

It is these children who have grown up and become freedom fighters. It is very rare for them to surrender. They fight to the end. The last words from their lips reverberate in the air – 'freedom' they say.

> *I vow to thee, my country*
> *All earthly things above*
> *Entire and whole and perfect*
> *The service of my love*

Cecil Arthur (1900)

Thousands of years of servitude and obeisance towards masters of repression and torture have made an impression on the minds of people. A spectre of freedom and liberty has haunted them for all those years and now, quite opposite to their beliefs and philosophy of life, they have armed themselves, opened their shirt buttons and are prepared to die with honour.

Laurels will always be laid for the estimated 45,000 people who have laid down their lives so far in the name of their nation. The future generations will remember them as martyrs with an indelible mark in their hearts for many years to come. For now the spectre of agony continues and one tribute the martyrs in Heaven will appreciate is the fight for freedom which will continue to the end.

*

1149, the poet and historian Pundit Kalhane stated in his *Chronicles*, "Such is Kashmir, the country which may be conquered by the power of moral excellence but not by armed force."

*

1210, "Throughout their history the Kashmiris have ranked among the foremost traders of the subcontinent."

John Bogle (East India Company)
Chronicle Of Exploration

*

June 5th, 1589, Father Jerome Xavier, a priest, accompanied Akbar and his massive invasion into Kashmir. He wrote in *Political Repression*, "The Kingdom of Caximir (Kashmir) is one of the pleasantest and most beautiful countries to be found in the whole of East. It is rich in natural resources, pastures, orchards gardens, waterways, countless springs, lakes and rivers but with cruel irony Kashmiri people are starving."

*

1605, "Kashmir is a garden of Eternal Spring." wrote Nur-ud-Din Jahangir. The last words on his lips before he died, were "Kashmir only Kashmir."

*

1665, Dr Francois Bernier, the Frenchman who travelled extensively, said about Kashmir, "Kashmir will become the focus of the Asiatic civilisation. The very rich norms of art and culture and teachings of literature will permeate into the subcontinent from Kashmir. It is a historical fact that the subcontinent should look up to Kashmir, Jammu and Ladakh for inspiration and refinement of all religions."

He also said that "The people are celebrated for their wit and are considered much more intelligent and ingenious than the Indians."

*

" ...until 1886 it was a completely independent state, maintaining its own diplomatic relations. It received no British residents in its courts."

(Dr K.M. Panikkar)

*

1892, Walter R. Lawrence

"It is a matter of surprise that under a rapid transition of governments, varying in race, religion, and language, the people of the Valley should have retained their peculiar nationality un-impaired." ... "Facts will be found which will show that 'crime' is almost non-existent in Kashmir."

*

May 15th, 1934, Wardha; Letter from Mahatma Gandhi, addressed to Mr Prem Nath Bazaz.

"Dear Friend. I have gone through your paper. We are sowing as we have reaped. Seeing that Kashmir is predominantly Mussalman [Muslim] it is bound one day to become a Mussalman state. A Hindu Prince can therefore only rule by not ruling, i.e., by allowing the Mussalmans to act as they like and by abdicating when they are manifestly going wrong. This is the ideal. What is expedient is more than I can judge.

Yours Faithfully   M.K. Gandhi."

*

"The men and women of Kashmir are good to look at and pleasant to talk to. They are intelligent and clever with their hands. They have a rich and lovely country to live in. Why then, should they be so terribly poor?"

Pandit Jawaharlal Nehru.

*

1947. Cyril Radcliffe, the architect responsible for the mechanics of dividing India into India and Pakistan, pencilled in the two crucial Eastern districts of Gurdaspur, a Muslim majority city to be included in the Indian dominion. The implications of this action were that India established a road link into Jammu and Kashmir through Gurdaspur. Political analysts have stated that "The Kashmir dispute would not have existed if Radcliffe's pencil did not waver into that scroll."

*

King George V proclaimed: "My determination is ever to maintain privileges, rights and dignities of the princes of India. The princes may rest assured that the pledge remains unimpaired and inviolable."

It is ironic that his own nephew oversaw the violation of these princely states, as in Junagargh, Hydrabad and Kashmir.

*

October 27th 1947.

"My Dear Maharaja Sahib,

Action has been taken to send troops of the Indian army to Kashmir to help your own forces to defend your territory and to protect the lives, property and honour of your people.

I remain, Yours sincerely

Mountbatten of Burma"

*

1947. "Hari Singh had packed his jewels, Persian rugs and paintings; gathered his concubines and fled to Jammu. Accession to India was thus done under pressure."

(Pranay Gupte, *Mother India, (Biography of Indira Gandhi).*

*

July 27th, 1948. "Britain's past pledges to the princes [of British India] entitled Kashmir and Hydrabad to choose their own future by a plebiscite on the basis of adult suffrage."

Winston Churchill to Lord Atlee, prime minister of Great Britain.

*

February 8th, 1950. "Kashmir is being treated as a pawn in the game of power politics."

Daily India Tribune (S. Gupta)

*

April, 1952. "No one can deny that a communal spirit still exists in India. Many Kashmiris are apprehensive as to what will happen to them, if for instance Nehru dies! Indian attempts at applying Indian constitution in Kashmir are unrealistic, childish and smacking of lunacy."

Sheikh Abdullah making a speech in Rambirsing, Pora.

*

1958. Percival Spear (author-historian-teacher in Delhi and Cambridge), speaking on the transfer of power by the British to Gulab Singh through the Treaty of Amirtsar in 1846 stated that: "The effects of this ill-omened act have not yet ceased to operate."

*

December, 1961. "The military approach, that is, any kind of warlike action *is alien to our culture* and tradition. In fact, we want the use of force *outlawed*. The means employed are as vital for us as the ends they serve. That is what Gandhi Ji taught us."

Jawaharlal Nehru (after the invasion of Goa)

*

August 14th, 1965. In the *Washington Post*, Selig Harrison reported after his visit to Kashmir: "I found the sentiments of the people almost solidly hostile to the Indian rule and that only the presence of twelve Indian army Brigades kept the movement of self-determination contained."

The people of Kashmir have always been lied to. In the light of this Joseph Goebels has said: "Keep on repeating the lie. Ultimately people will believe it."

*

Thomas Moore, the Irish Poet, had never been to Kashmir. He wrote the famous series of oriental tales in verse, connected by a story in prose, *Lalla Rookh*. The 'frame' story tells of the journey of Lalla Rookh from Delhi to Kashmir.

> *'Who has not heard of the vale of Cashmere,*
> *With its roses, the brightest that earth ever gave.*
> *Its temples and grottoes and fountains as clear*
> *As the love-lighted eyes that hang over their wave.'*

A part of *Lalla Rookh* was written as a love story set in the Shalimar gardens. Shalimar is known in Europe as a romantic place and the best perfumes are named after it. "Pale hands I loved beside the Shalimar."

Thomas Moore became famous for his fictional story, *Lalla Rookh*, which had a resemblance to a factual episode: The Mogul king set off for Kashmir from India with a mass of people in the entourage. His daughter travelled on a decorated elephant. She was going to Kashmir to see the prince of Bacharia (Bukhara) in order to get married to him. The long journey was tiring and bored her immensely. She asked to be entertained. A Kashmiri youth volunteered and recited poems and jokes all the way through the journey. The princess fell in love with him. She was taken to the Shalimar gardens to see the prince of Bukhara. She fainted, fearful of the prospect of meeting the prince, and her love for someone else overwhelmed her. It was only when she recovered and saw the prince all dressed up and looking at her, that she was very happy and excited. The Kashmiri young man she was in love with was actually the prince in disguise! They were married in the Shalimar garden.

Foursome – Awesome

The four men stood like the bandy legs of a misshapen table, unstable, and incapable of being used, but a worthy commodity to look at. Lord Mountbatten and Pandit Jawaharlal Nehru were the props at one end, Maharaja Hari Singh and Sheikh Abdullah at the other. It may be safely said that if these men had not existed, Kashmir would not have been torn apart in the way it was. It was Mr Nehru who wanted Kashmir, but he could not have done it without the help of the others. The table is limping now and is not even much use to anybody in its present state. It is worth carving out a profile of these men, expressed in each case as a little poem:

194

The good looking Brahmin
With his roots in the valley
His mind and heart sharing
His passion and his craving
He poised in gusty streams
He dwelt in shifty dreams
He acted on, he played on
He defied on, reneged on
Covetous eyes, smiling face
His heart was in the right place
He left the scene, departed
Simmering issues, thwarted

Majid Siraj

Mr Nehru changed the politics of the subcontinent around Kashmir. He lost friends and a great deal of his country's wealth. He had to defy and deviate in order to hold out his stand on Kashmir. He also forgot that he may die. Just when a settlement was in sight he decided to depart. That meeting with President Ayub Khan never materialised. Alive today, he would not have ordered his forces to inflict injury and cause bloodshed in the streets of Kashmir.

Who is he?

An Englishman, a gentleman
His uniform trim and proper
Lord O Lord, Mount a Mountain
Forays Kashmir with his Batten
O King O Mighty have you a soul?
World of sighs, was that your goal?
A fair deal! not trick and treat
Scroll and sign an empty sheet
Yet Brutus was an honourable man
Dagger in the back, whenever he can

Majid Siraj

Lord Louis Mountbatten was the viceroy when he acted as the arbiter and peacemaker. There were many flaws in his appointment.

1. He ended his tenure as viceroy and accepted the job of Governor General of India while still sorting the partition out. He literally became his own party. He acted in a partisan way.

2. His main interest was the Navy and not politics. He rushed the job of dividing a big nation seven months before its time. He did not foresee the ethnic massacres and did nothing to prevent them.

3. He was the King's nephew and not accountable to anybody. He did not follow guidelines from the British government especially with regard to the princely states. He oversaw invasion after invasion of many independent states.

4. He designed the instrument of accession for Kashmir. A condition, that 'people will finally decide', was the last line. As an army man he should have known that military force once entrenched in any territory can be difficult to dislodge.

5. He rushed Radcliffe to divide India, post haste, ordered him to include Gurdaspur in India (for Indian access into Kashmir) and to isolate East Pakistan. He left the subcontinent in a mess, some say a disguised 'scorched earth policy' at the end of the empire and the effects are felt today.

Lion in a cage?

He was a man from grass roots
A tangle of burgeoning shoots
> *Casting and pulling at manacles*
> *used his craft of handling people*
Seething times, soothing times
Pain and struggle finishing lines
> *Trusting friends full of guile*
> *Tossing, tumbling in his style*
He lost Kashmir from his dreams
Pride and prudence bursting seams
> *'Land to tiller' his jewel in crown*
> *Schools and colleges up and down*
Games in politics, not his scene
Poise and sway, could have been
> *Defeated doctrines and an idealist*
> *Kashmir wanted a pragmatist*

Majid Siraj

Sheikh Mohammed Abdullah had 'Kashmir' burning in his heart until it consumed him. He spent many years of his life in prisons and set out to give the people a sense of purpose in life, an awareness of self esteem, denied to them for generations. He was endowed with charisma, possessed a towering personality, and enthralling voice in speeches. People felt safe with him. They cried, ready to die, and woe to the vanquished following his trail! He was fighting against the repressive rule of the Maharaja for sixteen long years, when the campaign suddenly aborted. There was no more 'quit Kashmir' slogan against Dogra rule. Events took over which changed the political scene. It was as if the Sheikh were sprinting in a race and the finishing line had been moved. The Maharaja, like other princes in India, would have evanesced into obscurity, in any event, but it was rather unfortunate for the people of Kashmir that the Sheikh was on the scene. He was actuated to shoulder a double-barrelled gun – one directed at the ruler and the other at Pakistan. The fact remains – India would have still sent its troops into Kashmir, even if the Sheikh had not been there or even if he had opposed it. They would have retained a quasi-rule, with Mahajan as prime minister, and would have administered Kashmir from Delhi. People were not prepared for a confrontation. August, 1947, the Sheikh was in prison. He had his comrades with him. He knew the goal posts had been moved. The future of the state was hanging in the balance. Mr Nehru had him released. The implications of that gesture could have been foreseen. This was the time he should have made a compromise with politicians like Ram Chand Kak, even if he was responsible for putting him in prison. This was not the time for personal vendettas or even ideological friendships. Maharaja Hari Singh openly wanted independence, possibly retaining his reign for his lifetime. Pakistan was antagonised by the Sheikh's party and instead of a united stand, leaders fell apart and became pawns in the hands of both India and Pakistan. Choudry Gulam Abbas and Sheikh Abdullah were at opposite ends with their political roots splayed and exploited. Pakistan would have retained the already agreed upon terms of telecommunications and transport with the state. Mr Ali Mohammed Jinnah had clearly stated that 'independence' was an option open to Kashmir on the basis of the Independence Act of India and the Princes of India Act, passed by the British government and subsequently endorsed by a proclamation of King George V and Winston Churchill.

The problem of the Sudhan revolt in Poonch and the tribal invasion could have possibly been averted. Even at this late stage, the Sheikh could have asked to be a witness at the signing of the accession by the Maharaja. He could have inserted conditions, like a time limit for forces to be in Kashmir and a date for a withdrawal. After all, it was only his friend, Mr Nehru, who was the man behind the show. Some friend! One might say. I have even come across cruel pedantic writers, who claim the Sheikh was a blood relation of Nehru! The Sheikh could have intervened between India and Pakistan openly to stop fighting over Kashmir and stop bloodshed in the streets of his homeland. There were lacunae in his inexorable sway of leadership. He was gullible, emotional, fiery, intolerant and vindictive; all the luxuries an ascendant mass leader can afford, but a fatal recipe for a working politician playing a significant role in people's lives. His speech at the UN on February 5th, 1948, was very blunt and undiplomatic: "No power on earth can displace me!" he said. He realised his mistake when he was put in prison by his best friend, Mr Nehru. He made another mistake by accepting the role of a demoted chief minister's job and forgot all about the treatment his people and the government had experienced. His 'Delhi Agreement', this time with Mr Nehru's daughter, Mrs Indira Gandhi, also turned out to be an unprecedented fake and culminated in ushering the lion back into his cage.

Stomach-ache? Or was it a fake?

A baby in Kashmir hungry and cold
The baby in Paris was in a nurse's fold
Molly and coddle, wrapped in gold
Prince was born, the world was told
Working and sweating a bob to earn
To pay for a prince, the money to burn
Drunk in stupor till eternity
People to him 'nonentity'
Hiding in vain with stomach-ache
Betrayed the nation for his own sake
Playboy prince, flees his throne
People to wolves, history has shown

Majid Siraj

Maharaja Hari Singh flaunted his wealth in London hotels on debauchery, while his people slaved away in bonded drudgery in order to get a meal at night. The British Indian department bailed him out from a blackmail episode in London. Partap Singh did not like him. He wanted Jagatdev Singh from Poonch to inherit the throne. The British installed Hari Singh because he would be easy to manipulate. Hari Singh was educated and westernised. Tourism and the exploitation of local products took a boost during his time. The British community in Kashmir transformed Kashmir into a tourist paradise, from houseboats to golfing, polo, trekking and water skiing. Hari Singh went along with the reform. The crunch came at the crucial time of a decision for the future of his state. He became, as historians call him, the 'Dithering Maharaja'. He had no experience in serious matters like politics. He had a chance to be brave and tell Mountbatten in the Trikka fishing lodge on that auspicious night when they were discussing the future of the state, that he wanted the sway of his people and to maintain the de facto standstill. Instead, he went to bed and faked a stomach-ache. He did not give that answer to the waiting Mountbatten. He put flames in the Poonch revolt and was responsible for the pogrom of the Muslims in Jammu. His actions provoked a revenge from Pathans on the other bank of the River Jhelum. He was short-sighted and gullible. There was a crisis and he let himself be beguiled by his ascendant priest. He could have treated all of his people equally, extended hospitality to Mr Jinnah when he came to Kashmir for his holiday, refused to dismiss his prime minister, Mr Kak, and negotiated a peaceful settlement of Kashmir with both India and Pakistan. He lost his throne, his riches, privy purse, dignity, and a place in the history of Kashmir.

*

Arts and Crafts in Kashmir

No one in the world can claim to have an edge over Kashmir's craft. Even children of five sit for months on end and create pieces of art in papier maché, shawls and embroidery, woodcarving and carpets, creating ineffable masterpieces.

> *"These are our works, these works our souls display*
> *Behold our works, when we have passed away!"*

*

The Great Poets of Kashmir

Kashmir is a fertile ground for talent. People living in desolate places have written masterpieces. There will not be room in thousands of books like this one to reproduce the works or their comments. To only mention a few, Gulam Ahmad Mahjur, whose poems have become symbolic of the Kashmiri culture, Abdul Ahad Dar Azad who wrote *Shikwai Iblis* and three volumes of the *History of Kashmiri Literature*. To name a few illustrious ones: Zind Kaul, Gulam Hassan Beg Arif, Dilsoz, Shams Fakir, Samad Mir, Ahad Zargar, Ahmad Batwari, Rahman Dar Pitambar Fani, all have left a treasure of Kashmiri classical poetry. People sit through nights to listen to wonderful classics of Niama Sahab, Swach Kral, Asad Paray, and the *Kashur Sargam*. Kashmiri talent has also excelled in Urdu and Persian poetry. The prominent names are Nadim, Talib, Dina Nath Mast, Ahad Azad, Maqbool Kralawari, Rasul Mir, Wahab Paray, Permanand, Prem Nath Pardesi, and many others. A special mention must be made of Haba Khatoon and Lala Ded, the women who have left an immortal treasure of classics.

The writers of Kashmir are the most gifted people in South Asia. Sheikh Abdul Aziz, Mohammed Yosuf Teng (*Sheerzana*) Ali Mohammed Lone (*Asi Ti Chi Insan – We Are Also People*). The others who have made a mark are Gulam Nabi Khayal, Akhtar Mohi-ud-Din, who won an award for his book *Seth Sangar* (*Seven Peaks*), Gulam Mohi-ud-Din Hajini for the many volumes of excellent books they have written.

The mystics of Kashmir, like Sheikh Nur-ud-Din Wali have left Kashmir with a treasure of classics which are so deep that each word will take a genius to comprehend.

Oh how much I miss the roses
in my garden back home.
The roses my grandmother planted,
My mother watered
and I loved to pick and smell.

Oh how much I wished my homeland
was like a red rose
I could plant it in a pot
and carry, wherever I go!

(Anon)

Grandma or a wolf?

The people of Kashmir have always been trusting and docile. It is not a surprise that they believed in the promises given to them by people of eminence. Each time they were beguiled perfidiously.

The anglers in their crafty way
cozen the fish to make them prey.
The poor fish will bite the bait
go for it and meet her fate!
Honest and poor, forever they came
Tossing and turning in a political game
The world over! It is all the same
Victims in mayhem take the blame
They lure them, love them all in name
Devour them, spiteful, feel no shame
They seal their lips, stamp their toes
ghastly prisons, everyone knows
Wolf or Grandma, who can it be?
Lovely big eyes – or teeth you see
Young ones of Kashmir, a meal for thee
O! Incubus, O! unkind, set them free!

Majid Siraj

EUREKA

A Veritable Dream

I have spent six long decades soul-searching for a blend of piety and peace, looking up to Kashmir to provide the means of ultimate bliss for everyone, admiring it with ineffable love and hoping it will receive me back in its lap one day, when the time comes.

> *I close my eyes, float and amble*
> *Exalted in heavens, not in a fable*
> > *Streams of milk and honey and more*
> > *Exuberance, radiance not seen before*

> Majid Siraj

It is my privilege to indulge in the luxury of a dream. I close my eyes and instantly come upon the magic carpet which takes me home. In my daylight revelations, I come to know of more crimes committed against the people in Kashmir, so it becomes a 'phantom of delight' to part with the agony for the night when I sleep. This must be an exercise gone through by millions of Kashmiris, living with the knowledge of today and hopes for a tomorrow. For me, reflections, nostalgia, emotions and the experience of living in the West, culminate on a daily basis, into a nascence of building castles and day-dreaming. Interaction with grass roots people in Kashmir and the élite alike, makes it clear that a 'vision' for Kashmir is a prevailing feature and they live it in their dreams. These reflections, idle they may be, make people want to live! I want to share in their experience. The invincible desire for all dreamers is to build a utopian paradise for their children and for themselves to live in!

Kashmir is an ethereal cruise liner where dreams come true all the time. I am a stowaway on this ship, witnessing its majestic exuberance on the waves and undulations.

> *Will life and living as beautiful be*
> *Kashmir it is, where else can be!*
> *'The spa, the air, the water as pure*
> *cool and fresh as ever before*
> *Springs, streams, meadows and greens*
> *Birds singing and fluttering in trees*
> *Open your eyes, sniff and breathe*
> *Clear blue skies and the earth beneath*
> *Kashmir, Kashmir, my beloved dream*
> *My heart is burning, my eyes gleam*

Majid Siraj

The ebullience in the spirit of youth we witness every day gives hope and spurs you on to see a future in the twilight. How could you cherish the miracle of the clean ecosystem of Switzerland, the organised ski slopes of Austria, unspoiled trout streams of Scotland, without first closing your eyes? In my dream I have seen all the noxious petrol fumes, dust and polluting gases vanish. I see a ban on petrol driven cars and scooters. All the slums have been cleaned up. Squalor and filth from the cities have disappeared. A glare in the atmosphere with no pestilence, no man-made diseases, no destitution and no crime, has emerged! The fabric of society has changed. People live in harmony, with no malice or prejudice, rich and poor, privileged or lower class, handicapped or robust, yellow or dark, saffron or green, they all have filed in for a common cause – 'Greater Kashmir' – a welfare state has started with enough for everyone to share. The standard of the technical education has been set at the highest levels without compromising the inherent cultural values. The family life is without strife, litigations and exploitation of vulnerable people by authority in law and order. The civil administration has been streamlined. Into flames have been thrown the age old 'files' which the *head clerks* feasted on like flies on greased paper. Computerised and 'simple' records are in place for the services of administration, easily understood and promptly provided. How wonderful to see corruption wiped out! And ruthless punishments imposed on those who sacrifice the interests of the nation for their personal ends.

I see a simmering flame of enthusiasm in people to generate capital and prosperity. The state coffers are spent on planned development. My exotic movements of self indulgence have been the 'fly wheel' technology. Trams, running at thirty miles an hour, carry the bulk of passenger transport, battery driven cars stopping at garages not for petrol but to plug in their batteries for a charge, or horse driven carriages and cycling tracks, are introduced for transport.

Power generation is at the top of my vision. Industry is flourishing to its maximum potential and all natural resources have been exploited. The vision of Kashmir, as the world will see it, is a 'health spa'. The ambient atmosphere in my dream is so clean that the angels come from Heaven to grace its habitat. Kashmir has become a blissful retreat for relaxation, a cure for the invalid, and a hope of happiness in life for its people.

My ideas about a national health service in Kashmir have stretched my imagination to its limits. It is a composite of high standard, modern and efficient service and it is available and free to all. All emergencies are picked up from a source within minutes and treatment is started outright. Hospitals are clean and spacious. The atmosphere is charged with dogged professional discipline.

Preventative medical aids are provided for every citizen, as a rule. The ultimate object is to produce and maintain a generation, robust and free from disease. *We have created a place for heroes to live in.* Talent in achievements, so far dormant, has surfaced in creating sports teams, games and intellectual challenges.

Corporations in all cities, free from the smell of brimstone, function efficiently and all roads are dust free and clean. All refuse is collected and disposed of. Kashmir will visibly become the largest demolition site in the world. All ludicrous buildings are pulled down, no matter who they belong to. The hillside houses and those along rivers are rebuilt to look spectacular with white and green facades. All of the architecture is laid out to blend in with the beauty of nature. There is a green aspect visible everywhere. All the bald hills and Kerewas and every available patch of land has trees and plants sown on it. The shabby looking shop fronts have been refurbished to blend in with a new look. We can afford (in my dream!) a few skyscrapers in all the big cities and all the offices and business centres are housed into them. The pressure on the space for planned housing is relieved.

Agriculture is completely modernised and the copious supplies of water are used by a network of irrigation canals and conduits to its best advantage. Land is reclaimed from swamps, marshes and dry patches. Most of all, in my dreams all energy requirements come from our hydroelectric projects, wind power and other environmentally clean sources. Electricity lights up every home, the streets, the holiday places and educational institutions. It runs a large network of industries related to forest products, agriculture, horticulture, animal husbandry, precision and art, etc. All products from Kashmir are booming in the world markets, even bottled spring water. Tourists from all over the world have filled all the hotels and trade is at its peak.

There is no smell of gun powder and the cities are clean from the military. The police are friendly Bobbies, beating about the bush in their beat, blowing their whistles like they used to in the past. There is no crime, no violence, no fetters and no felonies. There is no war of attrition between the people and between the people and administration. My thoughts were so alive to see a government of an ideal democracy that when I woke up to the realities of the day, I was shattered.

The treasury coffers have a tight string and are logically controlled, with the spending utilising the last penny of fiscal allocations for research, development, and the welfare of the nation. The experts are there to be used. I find that all educated young Kashmiris living abroad with their entire families have come home with a wealth of knowledge, experience and money. The administration is revitalised. It is new Kashmir.

The politically correct doctrines about civil liberties are trickling through in varying doses; albeit compulsory acquisitions of land and property wrongfully adopted have given these rights a temporary setback. Refurbishing a whole nation, its infrastructure and its fabric require hard decisions. Public education, to inculcate patriotic fervour and benefits of working for the nation, are indoctrinated. I know Finland, for example, would not be a rich country if grass roots people did not plant trees everywhere they could, because they know the tree gives them beauty and prosperity. The 'green revolution in Kashmir' is a national cry. Everyone is a participant in it. It has brought colour to the bald, denuded hills, fields and countryside. An abundant supply of *electricity* will be the *sand* with which my castle is made. The sand will need the *water* to create the mould. That water will be what the *political renascence* will provide when the nation has risen up in glory.

EPILOGUE

There is no doubt that the people of Kashmir have suffered miserably for many generations for no fault on their part. They are in a state of mayhem now, again for no follies attributable to them. They are being tortured, not with the aim of obtaining information, but to break down the self-esteem, personality and identity of individuals and to create an aura of terror in the society. Indian intelligence has penetrated into the fabric of the society through the renegade forces and have all the knowledge they need about insurgents and their whereabouts.

India and Pakistan are fighting their battles in Kashmir. India has turned on the civilians with vengeance and very harsh malevolent behaviour, in order to somehow sublimate its anger against Pakistan. They hope to eliminate insurgency and establish a pro-Indian rule in Kashmir. Pakistan is vanquished without a fight, in the belief that India is in a morass in Kashmir and will drain its resources.

They are both wrong, because the revolution is gaining support with every new martyr, which have averaged fifteen a day. It is an interminable struggle and will end only with a political solution. India is not getting weaker with its operations in Kashmir because it has docked all development programmes to finance the massive half a million of its front line forces in Kashmir. In the meantime, the people of Kashmir, used as a pawn, are caught up in vicarious retribution between the two sides.

A solution to the Kashmir problem is attainable. It is only the politicians who have introduced complexities in the dispute, for their own vested interests. India and Pakistan have to end hostilities against each other and shake hands as friendly neighbours. They must both loosen their grip over Kashmir and let its people find their own way to their destiny. Citizens of the subcontinent want it, Indo-Pakistan intellectual groups want it and all rights organisations have demanded a resolution of the conflict. It is not surprising that even the Indian army stationed in Kashmir have come to the end of their patience with this fiasco. The General in Command, Mr Daya Kishore Arya, addressing the Red Cross in Kashmir, stated, "The forces become the stick with which to beat the political, administrative and criminal justice system. The government becomes party to the breakdown of political and social order." It is never ending for them. The Rashtria Rifles regiment of the Indian army recently rescued a bus load of abducted journalists from the clutches of a terrorist group in Anantnag Kashmir. The press men were amazed when the army just turned up on the scene face to face with armed captors and asked them to release them. No arrest was made as it turned out that the terrorists were the renegade militants sponsored by India. These renegades have looted, plundered and murdered the citizens of Kashmir even more ruthlessly than the army itself.

Western powers will have to stop playing Machiavellian games and propping fractious democracies for petty gains and spur on the peace process. They must decide what is the correct position, and what is the best way to achieve a just solution and then impose their will. A far more difficult problem in South Africa was solved only with sanctions, a boycott of social, economic, sports participation and persuasion. The Kashmir problem is more amenable to resolution and has the ingredients to work on.

The violence has spilled into the cities of India and Pakistan. In the last few months, five bombs have killed and injured hundreds of innocent people in Delhi, Rajasthan and Lahore. The Kashmir dispute is spinning the subcontinent into destruction. India and Pakistan have to stop bellicose posturing and come closer to each other. Kashmir will drop out unscathed as a by-product of their goodwill and build on the foundations of laissez faire relationships with the rest of the subcontinent.

SELECT BIBLIOGRAPHY

Abdullah, Sheikh, *Flames of Chinar (Atishe Chinar)*, Translated by Khushwant Singh, Viking Penguin India 1993

Ahmad, S. Akbar, *Resistance of Control in Pakistan*, London, Routledge

Ahmad, S. Akbar, *Post Modernism and Islam*, London, Routledge

Akbar, M.J., *India the Siege Within*, UK, Harmondsworth, 1985

Akbar, M.J., *Nehru, The Making of India*, NY, Viking, 1989

Ali, Mooin Reza, Aijazuddin, Ahmad and Ali, Mohammed, *The Valley of Kashmir, 2 vol.*, India, Vikas Publishing

Baker, W. William, *Kashmir Happy Valley, Valley of Death*, LA, Defenders Publications inc., 1994

Bazaz, Prem Nath, *Truth About Kashmir*, Kashmir Democratic Union, 1950

Bazaz, Prem Nath, *The Crucible,* Delhi, Kashmir Publishing House, 1954

Bernier, Francis, *Travels in the Mogul Empire*, London, Archibold Constable, 1981

Brown, Judith M., *Modern India*, Oxford University Press, 1994

Collins, Larry and Dominique, Lapierre, *Freedom at Midnight*, London, Granada Publishing, 1981

Coupland, Reginald, Sir, *India a Restatement*, Oxford University Press, 1945

Dube, Mattoo, Suraiya *Kashmir, The Trefoil*, Delhi, Spantech Publishers, 1989

Farooqi, Mufti B.D., *Kashmir Cries for Justice*, Srinagar, 1991

Fergussan, J.P., *Kashmir, Historical Introduction*, 1961

Fishlock, Trevor, *India File*, UK, John Murray, 1983

Forbes, Rosita, *India of the Princes*, London, Trinity Press, 1939

Freedom House, *Freedom in the World*, London, National Book Network, Lanham

Gerivis, P., *This is Kashmir*, 1954

Gopal, Sarvepalli, *Jawaharlal Nehru, A Biography 2 vol.*, London, Jonathan Cape Ltd, 1979

Gupte, Pranay, *Mother India (Biography of Indira Gandhi)*, NY, Maxwell MacMillan International, 1992

Gupta, Sisir, *Kashmir, A Study of Indo-Pakistan Relations*, 1950

Gunnar, Myrdal, *Asian Drama, vol.3*, London, Penguin Books

Hamid, Shahid, *Disastrous Twilight*, London, Leo Cooper Co

Hanson, A.H., and Janet Douglas *India's Democracy*, London, Weidenfield and Nicolson, 1972

Hiro, Dilip, *Inside India Today*, London, Routledge, 1976

Hough, Richard, *Mountbatten, Hero of Our Time*, Book Club Associates 1980

Johnson, B.L.C., *India Resources and Development*, London, Heinemenn Edu. Books 1979

Kaul, Gwash Nath, *Kashmir Then and Now*, 1924, Rv. 1924

Keenan, Brigid, *Travels in Kashmir*, Delhi, Oxford University Press

Khan, Gulam Hassan, *Government and Politics of Jammu and Kashmir*, J.V. Printers, 1988

Knight, E.F., *Where Three Empires Meet*, 1893

Korbel, Joseph, *Danger in Kashmir*, Princeton University Press, 1966

Lamb, Christina, *Waiting for Allah*

Lamb, Alaister, *Disputed Legacy*, School of Oriental and African Studies

Lamb, Alaister, *Birth of a Tragedy*, Roxford Books, 1993

Lawrence, Walter R., *The Valley of Kashmir* (Reprint), Kashmir, Chinar Publications, 1991

Lowe, N. ed., *Modern World History*, Macmillan, 1982

Mehta, Ved, *Portrait of India*, London, Yale University Press

Menzes, S.C., *Fidelity and Honour*, Viking

Moore, R.J., *Escape from Empire*, Oxford University Press, 1983

Nossiter, D. Bernard, *Soft State*, NY, Harper and Row, 1970

Sharma, Dhirendra, *India's Commitment to Kashmir*, India, Philosophy and Social Action Publications, 1994

Stephens, Ian, *Pakistan*

Stern, W. Robert, *Changing India*, Cambridge University Press, 1993

Sufi, G.M.D., *Social, Political, Cultural and Religious History of Kashmir*, New Delhi, Light and Life Publishers, 1974

Sugarman, A., Martin *Kashmir: Paradise Lost*

Times of India Supplement, *New Kashmir*, 1962

Vigne, G.T., *Travels in Kashmir, Ledakh and Iskardo*, London, Colburn, 1842

Wolpert, Stanley, *India*, University of California Press, 1991

INDEX